"Cooperative, iterative, and long-term: that's what the authors of this fascinating book would like to see much more of in the world of education policymaking, and so say all of us! It is absolutely no surprise that my ex-colleague Gareth – along with Nansi – have written something so thoughtful, engaging and practical."

Jonathan Slater, *Former Permanent Secretary at the Department for Education, UK*

Improving Education Policy Together

By focusing on the relationships involved, *Improving Education Policy Together* will change how policy-making in education is approached and showcase alternative models that will lead to more sustainable and effective practices.

The authors analyse the state of educational policy-making in England. They particularly reflect on the relationships of the different people and organisations involved – policy-makers such as politicians, civil servants, and unions – and explain how these interact with the wider world. Building on the experiences of the authors on different sides of the process, the book explores the reasons why education policies fail the very sector they are intended to serve. By considering aspects of policy-making in different countries, the authors highlight more effective ways of building relationships between decision-makers and those affected by educational policy. This book explores, as an alternative, long term, systems-led, and relational policy-making, and maps out a range of unique models for change.

Of interest to those involved in developing and influencing policy in government, this book will be essential reading for political parties, unions, civil servants, and charities, as well as teachers and leaders who believe they should be much more influential in the policies that affect their working lives and seek to adopt a better approach to making education policy.

Nansi Ellis is a freelance education policy consultant and a school governor, formerly Assistant General Secretary (AGS) for the National Education Union and previously for the Association of Teachers and Lecturers (ATL), leading education policy development.

Gareth Conyard is co-CEO of the Teacher Development Trust (a charity providing professional development support for teachers) and was formerly a senior civil servant at the Department for Education.

Improving Education Policy Together

How It's Made, Implemented, and Can Be Done Better

Nansi Ellis and Gareth Conyard

Routledge
Taylor & Francis Group

LONDON AND NEW YORK

Designed cover image: Paolo Carnassale / Getty Images

First published 2024
by Routledge
4 Park Square, Milton Park, Abingdon, Oxon OX14 4RN

and by Routledge
605 Third Avenue, New York, NY 10158

Routledge is an imprint of the Taylor & Francis Group, an informa business

British Library Cataloguing-in-Publication Data
A catalogue record for this book is available from the British Library

Library of Congress Cataloging-in-Publication Data
Names: Ellis, Nansi, author. | Conyard, Gareth, 1978- author.
Title: Improving education policy together : how it's made, implemented, and can be done better / Nansi Ellis and Gareth Conyard.
Description: Abingdon, Oxon ; New York, NY : Routledge, 2024. |
Includes bibliographical references and index. |
Identifiers: LCCN 2024001550 (print) | LCCN 2024001551 (ebook) |
ISBN 9781032651040 (hardback) | ISBN 9781032650982 (paperback) |
ISBN 9781032651057 (ebook)
Subjects: LCSH: Education and state--England. | Education--Aims and objectives--England. | Educational change--England.
Classification: LCC LC93.G7 I67 2024 (print) | LCC LC93.G7 (ebook) |
DDC 379.42--dc23/eng/20240130
LC record available at https://lccn.loc.gov/2024001550
LC ebook record available at https://lccn.loc.gov/2024001551

ISBN: 978-1-032-65104-0 (hbk)
ISBN: 978-1-032-65098-2 (pbk)
ISBN: 978-1-032-65105-7 (ebk)

DOI: 10.4324/9781032651057

Typeset in ITC Galliard Pro
by Taylor & Francis Books

When an apple has ripened and falls, why does it fall? Because of its attraction to the earth, because its stalk withers, because it is dried by the sun, because it grows heavier, because the wind shakes it, or because the boy standing below wants to eat it? Nothing is the cause. All this is only the coincidence of conditions in which all vital organic and elemental events occur.

Leo Tolstoy, *War and Peace*[1]

[1]   Taken from Book Nine, Chapter 1 of the translation by Aylmer and Louise Maude, www.gutenberg.org/cache/epub/2600/pg2600-images.html#link2HCH0138

Contents

Acknowledgements

From Nansi: Thank you to Jonathan and Adam, who always make me smile: I couldn't have done this without your support. And thank you to my friends and colleagues who have challenged my thinking and put up with me as I've chased the new shiny things over the years – you know who you are.

From Gareth: Thank you to my family, who love me and have helped me through this and so many other endeavours: to Maria, Fred, and Annie, for your constant support and joy and to Jacq and Jason for first believing in me. And thank you to Hannah who helped to fix me.

Introduction

The English education system is complex and varied, with literally hundreds of thousands of people involved in the development and delivery of education policy, from the Secretary of State sitting in their office in Sanctuary Buildings in Westminster to the teacher planning next week's lessons at the kitchen table on a Sunday morning. Nobody should be under any illusions that making education policy is easy and any solution that seems to promise an obvious way forward should be treated with extreme scepticism.

But we should expect more than we currently have. In part as a reaction against the very complexity that it is necessary to navigate, for too long policy ideas and interventions have become too simplistic, focused on quick wins and headline-grabbing initiatives rather than considered ideas. The notion of putting in the hard work to understand evidence, to build consensus, and to invest in a proper cycle of implementation has been abandoned, replaced with the dopamine-hit acts of division and stubbornness. It has become a game of winners and losers at the expense of focusing on getting the best outcomes for children.

We are writing this book on the cusp of a general election. Within the next few months we may have a Labour government (if the polls prove accurate). Less likely, but still possible, is the return of a Conservative Party with nearly a decade and a half under its belt in power. And, of course, we should not ignore the possibility of a coalition government of one blend or another. Whichever party forms the next government, they will be inheriting an education system that has suffered from years of bad policy-making and funding, of gimmicks rather than solutions, of knee-jerk announcements instead of long-term, evidence-informed judgements.[1]

As all the parties draw together their platforms for government, fleshed out in the glossy pages of a manifesto, there will be no shortage of ideas for them to consider. The think-tank industry will churn out provocative and emotive policy papers, the success of which will be determined more by the influence and traction they gain within a political party than the positive impact on the education system. Lobby groups and thought leaders will be ramping up their efforts to be 'heard' by prospective ministers, unions will be working behind the scenes to take positions of influence, those hoping to be in positions of power within political parties will be setting out their stalls. None of this will be done without evidence – no think tank worth its salt would dream of publishing something that does not have

DOI: 10.4324/9781032651057-1

links to academic papers, polling data, and focus groups – but few ideas will be interested in a comprehensive understanding of the evidence with all its contradictions in a complex system. The idea will come before the evidence; the tail will wag the dog.

So, we should be clear from the outset that this book is not about offering any policy ideas. You will not find a quick-win gimmick anywhere in this book for the government – of whatever political hue – to provide more funding for any initiative or to create any new programme. Instead, we are interested in how policy comes to be made and delivered, what are the systemic issues that shape the process, and how they might be addressed so that we come to a better, less myopic place when it comes to improving the English education system. Without making fundamental changes to the way in which policy-making is developed and delivered, we will continue to be plagued by the same challenges and issues that have helped to create the challenging position so many schools now face. Good policy should be the norm, not the serendipitous accident it too often is.

This is not directly about any particular political party – the Conservatives, Labour, and the Liberal Democrats have all had their share of more or less competent ministers, attention-seeking initiatives, and short-term political trade-offs over the last quarter of a century and more – but any consideration of how to make better education policy cannot but be framed against the backdrop of Conservative-led governments since 2010 and the decisions they have made. So, although the Conservatives are likely to be referenced more in this book, it is because they are the incumbents (the price of power) rather than for any ideological or political reasons.

The first half of the book sets the context in which policy-making happens. We start in Chapter 1 by considering the role of the individual in policy-making and delivery. Education can be an intensely individual act, even a lonely one, and understanding why people think the things they think and make the decisions they make is an essential foundation. We then move on, in Chapter 2, to consider how those individual intentions and ideas are shaped by history and constrained by the systems in which we all operate – the role of parties, unions, and other education organisations in shaping the way that individual thoughts and actions play out. This is built on in Chapter 3 by starting to consider the complexity of the system and how that has an impact on the decisions that are made and – perhaps more importantly – on the efficacy of delivery. How do school curriculum choices interact with decisions around SEND or children's social care, for example, as well as wider government and societal factors. Chapter 4 reflects on more recent history to explain how the current world is shaped by recent efforts at collaboration, as well as division, with longer-term trends and expectations that can sometimes feel like an invisible hand shaping events against the best efforts of policy-makers.

In the second half of the book we consider how things could be different. Chapter 5 looks to the wider world to see what we might learn from international examples. Chapter 6 takes a different lens to see how diverse thinking approaches can help us consider better ways to make policy. These come together in Chapter 7 with some recommendations about the sort of policy-making system we think is needed to respond to the challenges the education system faces today – an approach that is more collaborative, iterative, and long term. Chapter 8 takes these abstract ideas and turns them into a practical toolkit that those involved in policy-making can use, a tangible way to turn the ideas we set out in this book into action. We finish, in Chapter 9, by taking an example through the toolkit to demonstrate how it might work in practice.

Our hope is that this book helps all of those involved in or interested in the development and delivery of policy to gain a deeper understanding of how the system currently works – the motivations and incentives, the barriers and constraints – that shape the decisions that are made. Using this understanding, we hope to provide different ways of thinking about and creating education policy so that it becomes more effective in the future, that outcomes are intended rather than accidental, and that more informed and considered judgements can be made.

Nansi Ellis and Gareth Conyard

October 2023

Note

1 See the CIPFA/IoG performance tracker for a record of the current state of public services: Stuart Hoddinott, Nick Davies, Matthew Fright, Philip Nye, and Gil Richards, *Performance Tracker 2023: Public Services as the UK Approaches a General Election* (Institute for Government & CIPFA, 2023). www.instituteforgovernment.org.uk/sites/default/files/2023-10/performance-tracker-2023.pdf

1   Why do people think what they think?

Education can be a fiercely individual endeavour. It is about a teacher at the front of the classroom trying to get through the complexities of a problem before the lunch bell rings, the child sweating over an exam in an eerily silent hall, the minister working through a red box late into the night after a day of meetings and press, making decisions affecting the lives of thousands. In each of these examples, we can see the importance of individual agency – people matter and the decisions they make have a direct impact on so many others, not least the children at the sharp end of the education system. So what shapes the decisions of individuals as they interact with education policy and delivery?

Education policy-making suffers because everybody knows enough about it to have opinions but not necessarily enough to make effective choices. We have almost all been to school, had a teacher that we love or hate, found solace in the pages of a book or dread at the prospect of a double period on a Friday afternoon. We are all able to extrapolate from our own experiences and those of people we know to create an idea of what better might look like.

It is a common question: who was your favourite teacher? Ours are Mr Walker, who taught history and who was able to really land the social, economic, and political dynamics of the interwar years in a way that made the complex intelligible (and who was able to challenge a cocky teenager to focus on the content rather than showing off in class), and Mrs Bradley, who taught English and who encouraged playing with language, engaging with what makes people come alive, and asking difficult and deep questions about the world.

These teachers helped to shape our thinking as adults – that is what teachers are meant to do – as did our wider school experiences. One of us was itinerant and went to three different primary schools, and two secondary schools, ending up at an all-boys grammar school in the heart of Kent, played rugby, and had a special tie as a senior prefect. He then went on to work as a civil servant in the Department of Education (DfE). The other went to a Welsh-language primary school next door to the English-language school, and then was in the second cohort of a new Welsh-language secondary school as South Wales grappled with its Welsh identity, played netball (rugby wasn't available to girls), and competed in the Eisteddfod. She also became a primary school teacher herself, before working on education policy in government agencies and unions.

DOI: 10.4324/9781032651057-2

These experiences obviously have an impact on what we remember as good and the policy issues we might think are priorities. It isn't, to be clear, a direct cause-and-effect – going to a grammar school doesn't mean that you will support grammar schools – but our experiences nonetheless shape us. The questions are do we recognise how, and do we adjust to ensure we are not letting biases overrule facts?

For most involved in education, our past experiences and the way they shape us are benign or positive influences. Most people need to engage with education as a student or a parent. They need to know enough to build relationships with teachers and schools and to navigate the balance between education and the wider pressures of life. In these circumstances, reflecting on our own education experiences can be a boon, helping the parent empathise with a child in the middle of exams, or reaching back to remember that feeling of support engendered by a caring and supportive primary school teacher and reflecting that back at a parent's evening. It can also, of course, be a distinct disadvantage; remembering the feelings of inadequacy at subjects not understood, being made to think that your face didn't fit, or believing that education had no bearing on the life you were destined to lead can be reflected in a parent's confidence to engage in the system at all and their capacity to support their own child to navigate it.

For most teachers, holding a view based on childhood experiences is generally okay, having only a tangential impact on the way that education is delivered in most circumstances. It won't impact on funding, statutory requirements, curriculum expectations, etc. It can, of course, have a profound impact on an individual pupil (there are good reasons why we remember the teachers we like and also the teachers who had a negative impact on us), and even reach across a school in terms of things like ideas about behaviour or curriculum. It can also have an impact on the willingness of a teacher to consider contrary ideas and respond to challenges and changes. But it won't shape the wider system and won't impact on teaching colleagues outside of immediate relationships.

But what about those people who are in a position of wide systemic influence? Ministers, civil servants, union general secretaries, leaders of professional bodies? Every new Secretary of State for Education is profiled in the sector press, and their own experience of schooling is a key part of this. Were they privately educated? Did they go to university and, if so, where? Who was their favourite teacher and why? All this is done to look for clues as to how they might react and what policies they might pursue.

Many a union conference has suggested that an education minister should spend a term in a classroom, in order to understand the day-to-day life of a school. This is not to suggest that those with school experience are necessarily best placed to lead education policy development. Estelle Morris was a teacher before she became Schools Minister and then Secretary of State under Tony Blair. She was well respected by large sections of the profession, but in her resignation letter was very clear that she did not have the skills to manage a large department or to deal with the media.[1] Some might say this is true of many others, who perhaps don't have the honesty or the self-knowledge to say so. More recently, Jonathan Gullis, previously a teacher before a brief spell as Schools Minister, went on the offensive at Education Questions in Parliament against what he called 'woke warrior teachers' who were pushing 'extremist nonsense' onto pupils, wanting to 'cancel important historical figures such as Sir Winston Churchill', and suggesting that they were 'aided and abetted by some trade unions such as the National Education Union'.[2] Having been a teacher is no guarantee you will make a good education minister.

Let us consider how the experiences of these key decision-makers shape the decisions they make – as individuals influencing and working within a system – in two ways. First, we can think about the formation of beliefs, the inputs that explain how people involved in education policy-making carry the baggage they all carry. These are based on cognitive processes that are common to everybody, not just those working in education. Second, we can consider how those beliefs respond under the circumstances faced by key decision-makers – how they play out when dealing with some of the actual issues that are faced when making education policy and seeking to implement those ideas.

The formation of beliefs: the inputs that shape us

Mental models

Our upbringing, our experiences of school, the people we listen to, the books and the media we read all combine to build our mental models of the world. The idea of 'mental models' was proposed in 1943 by psychologist, Kenneth Craik, who suggested we all carry in our heads a 'small scale model of how the world works'.[3] It is very difficult to hold a large number of unrelated facts in our heads and so we build a framework on which those pieces of information can sit. We use these mental models to make sense of the world, and to shape the way we make decisions and the way we learn. While these are personal to us, psychologists also talk about collective, or cultural, mental models: a group of people internalise their shared experiences, creating cultural meaning that influences the ways in which they relate to the world. As we specialise, and join more specialised groups, our mental models are likely to become more specialised too: engineers may see the world in systems, biologists in terms of evolution, economists in terms of efficiencies. In education terms, we might call these 'schema'. Our mental models influence what we believe about education and how we think the education system works.

Of course, our mental models are not complete pictures of how the world works; they are focused on those aspects that relate to our goals, our experience, our current knowledge. We use them to filter the information we take in: we may reject evidence that conflicts with our mental model or evidence that we can't make sense of. We often assume, often without realising, that other people have similar mental models, and we cannot understand why they do not come to the same conclusions as us when we look at the same evidence.

Indeed, one of the most powerful elements of a mental model is that we may not realise we are applying it at all as it will feel so obvious to us, opinion eliding into fact, as though any other way of looking at an issue is impossible.

The acclaimed American academic and writer Brené Brown talks about the use of narrative in mental models, by asking the question, 'what story am I telling myself?'[4] By this she means that our internal thought process, the voice in our heads, often follows a narrative track without realising it and that narrative is often not grounded in objective fact, although it can feel very real indeed. This applies to relationships (personal and professional) as well as decision-making. For example, in the recent government response to the RAAC situation,[5] the Secretary of State for Education, Gillian Keegan, was caught in a 'hot mic' incident in which, following the end of an interview with ITV on the subject of the government's response, she said: 'Does anyone ever say, you know you've done a fucking good job because everyone else has sat on their arse and done nothing? No, no, no signs of that, no?'[6]

Setting aside the political and reputational impact of the incident, it offers a revealing suggestion for the mental model that Keegan was employing as she responded to the RAAC issue – the story she was telling herself is that she was having to clean up somebody else's mess and she was underappreciated for the efforts she was making. We will not attempt to speculate on the formative experiences that led Keegan to that internal mental model but they exist.

Cognitive biases

Cognitive biases are based on evidence of the way that the brain processes information, and in particular how that information is brought to bear when it comes to decision-making. Perhaps the best articulation of this is captured by the Nobel Prize winning academic and author Daniel Kahneman. In a seminal 1974 work (completed jointly with Amos Tversky) he investigated the unconscious beliefs – or heuristics – that shape intuitive decision-making;[7] you might think of these in terms of 'gut instinct'.

These ideas are unpacked in Kahneman's 2011 work, *Thinking Fast and Slow*,[8] in which he draws our attention to two parallel cognitive processes occurring when judgements are made and decisions taken. The first (which he refers to as system 1) are the unconscious, automatic cognitive processes that help us understand the world, that enable us to make immediate and unthinking judgements. These might include simple calculations (2+2) or driving on a quiet and familiar stretch of road. Although these both involve decision-making, that happens on an unconscious level as it is familiar and mentally easy. The second (which he refers to as system 2) are the conscious, deliberate attempts to apply thought to a process. These might include more complex calculations (he suggests 17×24 as generally of sufficient complexity) or overtaking a lorry on a busy stretch of motorway during a rainstorm.

These two systems operate seamlessly in most cases, helping all of us navigate a world of dizzying complexity, with 'system 1' cognition operating without us generally being aware, employing shortcuts to filter out and process information, and 'system 2' cognition being employed deliberately in more complex environments. There are several important points from Kahneman's work to bear in mind.

The first is that the scope and scale of 'system 1' thinking covers the majority of our daily cognition in ways that might not even occur to us. In particular, we make unconscious judgements about ideas and people without necessarily understanding why. A good example might be how we respond to somebody based on how they look, either because they share physical characteristics with somebody we have interacted with in the past (either positively or negatively) or because they are generally attractive.

The second is that it is possible for deliberative cognition to override unconscious cognition, but it is effortful. We can override an action based on an automatic, fearful thought – for example, if we hear the growl of a lion, we can force ourselves to stay put rather than run away – but that does not stop the automatic thought presenting and it takes a real effort to impose a deliberative response on top of an intuitive one.

The third is that 'system 2' thinking is by itself effortful and can blind us to other things occurring around us. A good example, building on one mentioned above, is the cognitive load required to focus on driving on a busy motorway in the rain, which is likely to prevent the driver from being able to pay attention to a conversation with a passenger that would be easy to engage with if driving on a quiet, familiar road. It is not just that it might be hard to concentrate on the conversation in busy traffic, but that the driver can be unaware that somebody is even talking to them.

Although clearly these cognitive processes are relevant for everybody, taken together, these different elements of cognition play out in the way policy-makers act.[9] An obvious example is the so-called 'Halo Effect' – the cognitive bias somebody unconsciously has ('system 1' thinking) based on how another person looks.[*]

Another good example is to consider how somebody might unconsciously judge the benefits of action or inaction – what can be referred to as 'action bias' or 'present bias'.

If you have ever decided to have that extra glass of wine and hang the consequences, or to stay in bed where it is warm rather than get up and go for that run, you have experienced present bias – you are prioritising the immediate rather than acting, even if the evidence supports action. In economic terms, once you have enough money for the necessities of life, it is much more fun to spend now than to put money in your pension. Decisions that have an immediate consequence are much easier to make and sustain than those when the consequences are longer term and probably more uncertain. Linked to this is 'status quo bias', where we hold firmly to what we know and resist any change, even when the need for change is overwhelming.

---

[*]   Although not the main focus in this section, it is worth reflecting on how these ideas are sometimes misrepresented (often deliberately) by those pushing a particular agenda around 'wokeness'. The 'Halo Effect' is a good example of an uncomfortable truth for those suggesting that systemic racism is not present. We are all subject to the 'Halo Effect', all inclined by virtue of our psychology to be drawn towards those who are familiar and to be wary of those who are not. That is no more contestable in the name of 'anti-wokeness' than climate change denial is when considering environmental policy. The only real question is how far it is acknowledged and acted upon.

At the other end of the scale, 'action bias' pushes us to want to do something rather than nothing. When there is a penalty in a football match, the goalkeeper is much more likely to dive to the left or the right than to stay in the middle of the goal, even though data suggest staying in the middle may be more successful.[10] There is both a bias to action on the part of the goalkeeper and the knowledge that staying central and not saving the penalty will lead to ridicule from fans. There is also a link to the idea of 'optimism bias' – the unconscious belief that a more positive scenario will play out rather than the most realistic one based on evidence. Indeed, Kahneman himself notes a number of public policy examples when explaining this idea, such as the cost of building the new Scottish Parliament building, which soared from an estimated £40m in 1997 to £109m by 1999. At its completion in 2004, the final cost was roughly £431m.[11] He labels this public policy impact of optimism bias as 'The Planning Fallacy'.

We should not assume that such biases are immutable and there are clear cases where they might change, again unconsciously. Let us consider the former Minister for Schools, Nick Gibb. Before the 2010 election, and immediately after taking office, he had a clear motivation to push for change, both for political reasons and – in Nick Gibb's case – for reasons of genuine ideological belief. However, as he spent more time in office, and more of his ideas made their way into firm policy and became part of the everyday experience of schools and teachers, it is unsurprising that he was likely to be inherently defensive about the choices he made and to look for ways in which the status quo is in fact correct, even where evidence suggests the contrary. He moved from 'action bias', in which he felt doing something was essential, to 'status quo bias', in which he was motivated to defend the current state of education, perhaps regardless of the evidence.

Values

Also impacting on our decision-making are our values. These differ from cognitive biases in that they are more consciously drawn, even if shaped by our wider experiences and the unconscious mind. It is common for most organisations to set out organisational values as overt statements for how they will operate and how they should be judged. Linked, but separate, are the actual values that those working for an organisation see playing out, which may often feel very different from those stated as fact. It is very common for an organisation to have a value around inclusion or diversity, for example, and yet that does not mean it acts in a way that makes all employees feel equally included. How content we may feel working in an organisation will often be linked to how far that organisation has values (or more importantly, lives up to those values) that align with our own.

If we think about our values as our individual, fundamental beliefs, it helps us to understand how we combine the conscious and unconscious – Kahneman's system 1 and system 2. The creation of a core value in the policy-making sense occurs as unconscious beliefs meet with a conscious thought process to define a worldview or ideology in abstract terms. As an example, let us consider the debate around the death penalty. Two people may both start with a clear and strong internal belief that doing harm to others is wrong, but come to different conclusions about how that should play out in the real world. One may say that because doing harm to others is so wrong, those who perpetrate such actions should be subject to extreme punishment, including death in some circumstances. Another may say that because doing harm to others is so wrong, they could never support any action that does significant harm, even if that is against a person who has harmed others.

There are many such values that people hold that influence how they may approach policy-making: for example, how far do we think that all people have equal value? That everyone is entitled to their beliefs and views? Do we value freedom of speech over community cohesion? Do we believe in unfettered freedom of choice or are there contexts in which that choice should be limited?

Our personal values can become crystallised in political values, frequently led by broad, tribal labels (socialist, liberal, conservative, nationalist, etc.) that can serve as shorthand for both our values and our decision-making. Opposing parties have different political values, with education becoming a battleground between ideas of private good, where benefits accrue to individuals, and public good, where benefits are to be enjoyed by society; the ideas of a 'meritocracy' where individuals succeed on their own merits, where you can 'pull yourself up by your bootstraps', or the belief that people's circumstances constrain or enhance their opportunities, that some have further to 'pull themselves up' or more obstacles in their way. The idea that every young person should be able to demonstrate their strengths and abilities becomes the notion that 'all should have prizes'; that education should be about sorting and rewarding people according to their achievements and that some achievements are worth more than others. Education values, and political ones, shape the problems that we see in education and the solutions that we believe are needed.

For example, when 'zero tolerance' behaviour policy began to take hold, there were many teachers who were comfortable with the 'broken window' theories that underpinned it.[12] In classrooms, this translated as making sure that even seemingly small transgressions – such as forgetting a pen or having the wrong shoes – had consequences, in the belief that being lenient for one was a form of unfairness and that it would signal that other rules could similarly be ignored. Other teachers were less convinced. Those who believed that children's circumstances throw up obstacles were concerned that they were punishing pupils whose families were less able to support them, or those with special needs, for behaviours they were not able to control. Those who worked with younger children who believed that good school behaviours take time to develop wanted more freedom to support children whose verbal development meant they were more likely to snatch a toy than ask nicely for it, rather than being expected to sanction that child. Those differences in view are in part explained by the individual values of the teachers who were enacting the policy – those whose values aligned with the government policy would find it positive, whereas those whose values did not may have been distressed.

Responding: when beliefs hit reality

Thus far, we have considered how the formation of individual beliefs occurs and how some of those beliefs might form within the education policy context. That takes us so far in beginning to understand why individuals act the way they do, but it is not the complete picture. It is also important to consider the specific circumstances that individuals find themselves in and how that experience has an impact on decision-making. In other words, what happens to individual decision-making when the baggage carried from the past makes contact with the present? How do cognitive biases play out in practice and abstract values translate into policy decisions?

Circumstances

One of the overlooked elements of policy-making is the actual, day-to-day experience of policy-makers in all parts of the system. Policy is not made in a vacuum and seldom made in a clear and calm environment, and even those with power and agency nonetheless have to navigate their context. Some of the challenges they face will be the result of the systemic operation of the education system (which we look at in Chapter 2) and the interaction between different, complex policy areas (which we look at in Chapter 3). But they also have to experience the very human and individual facts of life. Policy-makers are human, and might be more or less likely to make a particular decision based on their blood sugar level as much as the merits of an argument.

Let us start by considering those generally viewed as being at the top of the policy-making and delivery process – politicians. It is important to say up front that we are talking about politicians rather than politics here. This is not a discussion of the relative merits of different political parties – we have experience of all three major parties operating in government and opposition and these reflections apply equally.

If you are the new Secretary of State for Education and you walk into Sanctuary Buildings (the head office of the Department for Education in Westminster), how do you begin to understand your world, and how will the mental baggage you bring with you respond to the circumstances you find yourself in? What plans and ideas are likely to shape your decisions and behaviours?

First, you are likely to be guided by your party positions and the conversation you will have just had with the Prime Minister as she or he offered you the job. That conversation – typically brief in terms of the detail of the role – will cover a few key areas, things that will resonate with the public (or at least, that the Prime Minister and the wider Number 10 machine think will land well with the public), things that are getting media attention and need dealing with. There will not be a lot of detail in the conversation, and the manifesto on which your party was elected will be pretty thin on detail too. This is because these conversations and documents are not about policy but about politics – the art of projecting messages rather than the nitty-gritty of enacting change. Manifestos are about selling ideas at an election; they are not governing documents. So, immediately and very quickly you will have to start filling in gaps, bridging the distance between a brief and limited conversation and the immense responsibility you are about to take on. Already your brain begins to find ways to colour in the empty spaces between rhetoric and reality, leaning on exactly the sorts of cognitive processes we set out above.

Second, you will be guided by the more detailed briefings you quickly get from a number of places. You will have conversations with Number 10 policy leads and special advisors. Once you are able to appoint your own special advisors, they will begin to tell you what to focus on (and to be clear, few Secretaries of State get free rein with the appointment of their special advisors – Number 10 has to agree appointments). You will also be presented with a whole series of briefings from the civil service on what the urgent issues are (generally because of timing or money) and more detailed briefings about how the system works. This is a lot of information to take in, overwhelming amounts of data and ideas about things you would probably have no knowledge of or views on. So, again, you have to start trying to make connections, find ways of prioritising and understanding, insert yourself somewhere in the process in order to make it manageable.

Third, you will have to start forming relationships with your ministerial team and understand what their opinions, levels of knowledge, and motivations are. You might have incumbents with varying degrees of experience or neophytes dealing with many of the same challenges as you. Some will want to get your attention quickly, pushing their own ideas and ambitions; others may be more malleable which, in the earliest stages, can often mean being passive – waiting for your steers before forming their own views. Who do you listen to and why? Do you focus on their experience, their position in the party, those who say things that resonate with your opinions, those who look and sound most like you? Do you have a set of overt values that help you to navigate these relationships and help others position themselves with you?

Fourth, you will realise that your time is extremely limited. You are not just responsible for education policy but you have to play a wider role in the strategy and operation of government. You have to attend Cabinet and Cabinet Committees. You have mountains of paperwork to read. You have to represent the government in the media rounds and TV studios, knowing that you will be asked questions about whatever the hot topic is rather than your policy responsibility. What stories are you starting to tell yourself about your role and your responsibilities? Are you inspired by the chance to make a difference or overwhelmed by the amount of information? Do you feel humbled by the situation or know that you are the saviour the education sector has been crying out for? Are you excited by the opportunity or resentful of the burden?

Let us pause here for a moment to play out how this may have worked with the topical issue of RAAC noted above. Although we cannot be sure what Rishi Sunak asked Gillian Keegan to focus on when she was appointed as Secretary of State, we think it is extremely unlikely that RAAC would have been anywhere near the agenda. The same is true of any conversations Keegan would have had with her special advisors or the Number 10 policy leads. In fact, the first time it may reasonably have been brought to her attention would be as part of the introductory briefings from the civil service, in which she would have been told of many, many urgent issues that required her immediate attention and quick action. Those would include, *inter alia*, departmental budgets, legal cases, teacher pay, teacher sufficiency, decisions on SEND funding and future policy, PSHE guidance (including on transgender issues), internal staffing, FE funding and reform, HE funding, HE freedom of speech issues, early years sufficiency and funding, pupil absence, Covid-19 policy, etc. It would also have included briefing on capital issues, of which RAAC would be one issue amongst many. She may have asked her ministerial team to help her prioritise, to make sense of things, and the evidence seems to suggest that some conversations did take place (seemingly with Baroness Barran). But there is little realistic prospect of her fully grasping the consequences of the prioritisation decisions she had to make.

As we can see, against this confusing and fast-paced backdrop, you need some sort of frame of reference, some rubric to use to make sense of it all. This is where past experience comes in. If, for example, you are trying to understand how to make sense of industrial action in the teaching workforce, it is simply human to apply your own experiences to the circumstances. What do you think about teachers? Do you remember them being unhappy? Did their workload seem too much when you were a pupil? Do you think teachers are overworked and underappreciated, or do you think they have long holidays and a chip on their collective shoulder? In short – what are the stories you are telling yourself, what biases are beginning to colour your views, and what values are you applying to the decisions you are starting to make?

We then need to turn our attention to the people around the politicians – those special advisors, civil servants, general secretaries, sector group leaders, and policy influencers. Each and every one of those people will also be carrying the baggage of their own experiences of course, but they are likely to have the advantage of varying degrees of longevity over a new Secretary of State, and many will have at least some specialist knowledge or experience of education beyond their immediate, formative experiences.

Civil servants should be the most stable element of the government system. They are appointed on merit, remain in post regardless of who the minister is or even which party is governing, and frequently spend their whole career in the service, often in a single department. Their job is predicated on the fundamental principle of 'speaking truth unto power', of saying what needs to be said to a minister without fear or favour. But we have moved a long way from the principles of Northcote-Trevelyan,[13] and advancement in the civil service is now more closely linked to responding to political steers than ever before.

First, it is important to note that not all civil servants have the same functions. Across government, there are many thousands of civil servants in customer-facing and delivery roles, for example managing Job Centres or working as border security or passport inspection officers. Most civil servants do not interact much with the policy-making process at all, in fact, although it is a foolhardy minister who pushes an idea without understanding its impact on the ground, especially through the lens of the civil servants who work in their department.

The number of policy-making civil servants is comparatively small against the overall size of the service, although some departments have more, proportionately, than others. The Department of Education is one such department, as it has little in the way of operational delivery that it directly oversees. The roughly half-a-million teachers in England are not civil servants, for example. Even within a 'policy department' like Education, the seniority and role of different civil servants matters. According to the 2022–23 Departmental Report,[14] around 6,800 civil servants worked directly for the Department for Education, rising to around 13,000 if the agencies (such as the Standards and Testing Agency) and non-departmental public bodies (such as the Student Loans Company) are included. Of these 13,000 staff, just over 400 were reported as being in the senior civil service (or equivalent grade) – just over 3% of total staff – with perhaps as few as half of those leading policy teams. To be clear, a lot of policy development occurs below the senior civil service – with those at what is known as Grade 6 and Grade 7 particularly important – but the decision-making structure within the Department for Education – and other civil service departments – places the responsibility for actions at the feet of the relevant senior civil servant.

So let us imagine one such senior civil servant – a Deputy Director responsible for a team of anywhere between 30–100 people with a responsibility for a broad policy area (such as the teaching workforce, early years sufficiency, or school capital funding). Such an official might be new in post or may have been in place for some time (maybe even having been promoted from within the team now led), and may be dealing with an established minister or a brand-new incumbent. Clearly these factors will have an impact on how confident that official feels in terms of mastery of their subject and in how they are able to interact with more senior officials and ministers. Such a Deputy Director will be responsible for: a budget (typically in the hundreds of millions of pounds); the performance, well-being, job descriptions, and behaviour of all those in their team; understanding the policy area, including the detail of all relevant legislation, key issues and risks, history, controversies, and funding; forming and maintaining relationships with key stakeholders and opinion-formers across the system; building relationships with other civil servants with relevant policy briefs, including those in other government departments; delivering on existing commitments, including ensuring contractual requirements are met and spend meets fiduciary rules; and, there are always specific issues related to a brief (building codes, pension rules, child safeguarding, running a procurement, etc.).

We can quickly see that the idea that even senior civil servants are masters of their brief is a convenient lie for all parties. For the civil service, it creates the impression of control and stability; for ministers it creates a comfort (at least somebody understands the detail). In truth, although there are very many excellent and expert civil servants, the frequent moving of senior officials into new roles (generally every two to three years) and the fast pace of policy-making and delivery means it is difficult to be confident in developing a complete understanding of any policy area. The time to become an expert is – alas – more and more a myth in the civil service, although a lucky Deputy Director may have those working within their team who have been around for long enough to remember previous policy efforts. More importantly, we should not ignore how an individual might seek to navigate such a complex set of responsibilities, recognising how the breadth will quickly necessitate prioritisation using exactly the sorts of cognitive shortcuts and processes that ministers also apply. In particular, the pressure to be seen to be in control, to know your brief, is immense. No civil servant wants to look clueless in front of a minister nor to have to go back to the private office after a meeting and admit a mistake. How often does this lead a civil servant to stick to a line that is not supported by the evidence in order to save face?

This should not happen of course – the job of the civil servant is to speak 'truth unto power' even if that is uncomfortable, but that is not an accurate reflection of the nature of the job nor of the human motivations we all carry. Trite as it may sound, the sense of doing something that makes a difference – the value of service – is still a key motivation for many civil servants, something that is not possible unless you are able to be part of the 'in crowd' and to be respected and liked by ministers. This can create a pressure to say what ministers want to hear, something that has been exacerbated by a shift in the language used about the civil service in recent years, with the idea of 'serving the government of the day' emphasised over 'speaking truth unto power'. We would speculate that the key moment in that shift was the Brexit referendum, after which ministers have been increasingly likely to publicly criticise the civil service for being part of the 'blob',[15] and the turnover has increased of senior civil servants who seem to offer unwelcome advice to ministers. Good examples are the dismissal of Sir Tom Scholar from the Treasury when Liz Truss became Prime Minister in 2022,[16] or the dismissal of Jonathan Slater as Permanent Secretary of the Department for Education in August 2020.[17] Whatever the specifics of each case, the possibility that civil servants can and will be moved on if ministers are unhappy with them cannot but have the effect of making civil servants reflect on what they say, and what the personal consequences might be.

Moving briefly onto special advisers, it is hard to generalise about the personal experience they face because their routes into the role are so varied. Some will have genuine expertise in education; others will have none. Some will be linked to a minister (perhaps following a minister around Whitehall into different roles) and others will be appointments by Number 10 or the Party HQ. Some will have a specific focus on media and comms, while others will be asked to focus on policy. What is true for all is that they know they are amongst the most vulnerable employees in the system, being tied directly to the fortune of their minister, and they are asked to navigate a bewildering array of systems and organisations, not least the civil service department they have entered. Given this, it is no surprise that the effectiveness of special advisers is perhaps the most variable element of the system we have encountered – some are excellent, grasping their brief, reflecting their minister's wishes, helping take forward that agenda; others are ineffective, trying to influence an environment they struggle to understand.

Moving outside government, the world of teaching unions is also complex and varied. Traditionally, a General Secretary has come up the ranks of union activism, having been a union representative while teaching, and then taking local roles negotiating with the local authority over issues of conditions of service, being elected to the Executive, perhaps even being a former union President. In recent times, however, we have seen general secretaries who have come straight from school leadership, from leadership in initial teacher training, from leadership in the private sector and up the ranks of staff within the union itself.

In every case, the General Secretary must be elected by the membership. This begins with the selection process: a candidate has to be nominated by a number of local branches, or by the Executive, which means engaging with the important issues, but also with the people who have influence within the union. Meeting with local branches is a time-consuming process, involving travel across the country, which of course rules out a range of people for whom this is not an option. Only those who can garner sufficient support can go forward to the election itself.

These efforts do not necessarily mean that most of the membership has been engaged in the election process. Local branch meetings are often not well attended, and those who do attend are more likely to be activists than the majority of the teaching population. These days, hustings – where members can question the candidates – are often held online, which widens opportunities for more engagement, but most union members are unlikely to attend. A General Secretary can be elected on a very small proportion of membership. In the most recent election to the role, the NEU General Secretary was elected on a 9% turnout.[18] In 2019, the NASUWT General Secretary was elected unopposed, having been selected by the Union Executive, with his only challenger failing to gain the 25 Branch nominations needed to stand, meaning that there was no need for members to vote at all.[19]

What does this mean for the relationships that underpin policy-making? Those who become influential may win their position by appealing to a small proportion of vocal activists. They are successful because they articulate some very specific ideas that resonate with members who are motivated enough to vote. Sometimes they are elected because of their opposition to a policy of another candidate or party, making the election a divisive 'us and them' event which is then carried into their policy-making. And while general secretaries are usually elected for a fixed term, they can stand again, usually as often as they like. It is possible that if they fail to keep their Executive members on side, the activists could bring someone else in as their preferred candidate, but it is vanishingly rare for someone to stand (successfully) against an incumbent General Secretary. And when a General Secretary stands down, the next person in the post will not necessarily be someone whose approach aligns neatly with what has gone before.

When people meet policy

We will finish this chapter by reflecting on how the individual baggage each person brings to the policy-making process, and the personal circumstances they face, can have an impact on the policy decisions they end up making.

We have lost track of the number of times we have heard Secretaries of State and ministers revert to their own experiences and biases as they try to understand an issue. One example (without naming names) is a conversation with a Secretary of State about recruitment to teacher training: looking at another year missing the target for Modern Foreign Language (MFL) teachers, the decision over whether to increase the bursary was under consideration, and the response (paraphrased) was 'In my experience, you can do a lot in the world without learning other languages. I have never had a problem being understood – so many people speak English.' A good example of bias and belief triumphing over data and need. And we have lost count of the number of times that ministers, on being asked about the future of exams, call on their own experience of (mainly successfully) sitting exams in their explanations of why it is unnecessary to change a system that 'works'. It is clear that the personal experiences we all bring with us cannot help but colour our views and decisions. It does not necessarily follow that you automatically seek to duplicate your own experiences (especially if they were negative for you), but nobody can escape their individual circumstances without significant mental exertion.

Sometimes this can be a boon for a policy area. After Michael Gove became Secretary of State in 2010, he oversaw a significant programme of efficiencies in the education and children's social care system, all as part of the wider programme of austerity led by the Chancellor, George Osborne. During this period, the proportion of children in need remained largely static, but the proportion of looked after children increased by roughly 3% as overall spending on children's social care fell by 9% in real terms.[20] At the same time, Gove led a number of specific interventions intended to improve adoption rates,[21] which were reflected in the spend on adoption which rose from £247m in 2010–11 (in 2015 prices) to £344m in 2013–14 (in 2015 prices).[22] In other words, spending specifically on adoption rose significantly even as overall spending on children's social care fell. This may well be entirely the right policy – adoption is often a very positive outcome for a child, better than other outcomes within the children's care system – but it is notable that Michael Gove himself was adopted. How far can we disentangle Gove's personal experience from the hard evidence driving decisions? And, from the perspective of the adoption system, especially those children adopted – does it matter?

A Secretary of State looking at curriculum reform would do well to reflect on their own experiences and the baggage associated with them to check whether that is skewing judgement. What emotions does the memory of feeling inadequate in struggling through a period of double physics give them? Does that make them want to change the content of the curriculum, moving from far less instruction from the front ('Dr S— was so boring!') to more practical work? Or is there a feeling of inadequacy that makes them want to avoid any sense that they feel uncomfortable with a knowledge-rich approach? Neither instinct is automatic from the experience, but understanding how the experience may be colouring judgement helps to ensure that baggage does not overcome evidence.

Another important factor when considering how our instinctive responses may play out is to remember that education is a long-term endeavour – both in terms of the time it takes for most policy ideas to have a tangible impact and of course in terms of how it is experienced by the child as they progress from early years, through the schools system, and into further and higher education. And yet, politicians and most others involved in determining policy have a short time in which to make a difference. This can unconsciously lead to a focus on short-term ideas. For example, it is much easier to decide to make maths compulsory to 18, where the effects will be seen as soon as the first cohort of 16 year-olds must continue to take maths, than to refresh the maths curriculum in primary school where you will not know if 16-year-olds are better at maths for ten years or more. In the terms described above, this is a form of present bias – making a policy decision based on whether it will have an impact that benefits you in the short term over one that may have more substantial but deferred benefits. Or it might play out in a decision to do something – anything! – to demonstrate that you are responding to an issue, even if that response is unlikely to have an impact. Attendance rates becoming an issue, likely through a combination of the gradual breakdown of the social contract between parents and schools, exacerbated by the pandemic and the wider effects of poverty and underfunding of children's services?[23] Float balloons about fining parents more or removing their benefits,[24] and announce four new Attendance Hubs![25] In this example, something is seen as better than nothing, even if there is little clear evidence any of the ideas will actually deal with the underlying issues and lead to better outcomes.

We may recognise 'commitment bias' in our politicians and policy-makers too. We are likely to remain committed to an idea, or a policy, even when it becomes apparent that it is not the right path. We like to believe that we are rational decision-makers and that our decisions are based on good evidence, and on an accurate view of the world. We also like to believe that we are consistent. To change our minds about a decision might suggest that our worldview is wrong, or that we chose to focus on the wrong evidence – or even that we're not very good at making decisions. In order to 'save face', we may double down on our original decision, refusing to listen to arguments against it or becoming increasingly dismissive in the face of any opposition. Again, our political system does not help: politicians who change their minds, who accept that they were wrong, or who acknowledge new evidence are accused of 'u-turns', of 'flip-flopping' and of not being competent enough to govern. In order to overcome this, politicians and other policy-makers need a degree of bravery – to accept vulnerability – which can require a supreme personal effort. In the next chapter we talk about how organisational dynamics can make such acts even more difficult.

Chapter summary

- It is important to start by recognising that policy-making and delivery is led by individual people – a teacher in the classroom, a union leader on a picket line, a minister at the despatch box.
- So it is also important to understand why individual people think the things they think and make the decisions they make.

- This starts with a recognition of how the brain works to process information, forming the mental models, unconscious biases, and values that help those involved in policy-making and delivery navigate a complex world.
- It is then important to have an understanding of what the policy-making environment feels like to the people operating in it – what does it feel like to be a brand-new Secretary of State for Education?
- By understanding these factors, we can begin to see the baggage that people bring with them when considering evidence and options, and making decisions.

Notes

1 www.theguardian.com/politics/2002/oct/23/labour.publicservices
2 https://schoolsweek.co.uk/six-facts-about-new-dfe-minister-jonathan-gullis/
3 www.jstor.org/stable/bf20735c-fa3d-383d-85df-b1c08ed9732f?seq=2
4 See, for example, Brené Brown, *Rising Strong* (Vermillon, 2015).
5 Reinforced Autoclaved Aerated Concrete (RAAC) is a building material in use between the 1950s and 1990s with a limited lifespan of maybe 30–40 years, used in many public buildings including schools. In the summer of 2023, the advice on the safety of buildings using RAAC changed, meaning a number of schools previously deemed safe to occupy were no longer so deemed, and the Department for Education began the school year by closing a number of schools and fighting a rearguard action in the media to explain the circumstances and response. More at https://educationhub.blog.gov.uk/2023/09/06/new-guidance-on-raac-in-education-settings/
6 www.youtube.com/watch?v=kIXmtsDRcic
7 *Science*, Volume 185, 1974 (reproduced in full in Daniel Kahneman, *Thinking Fast and Slow* (Penguin, 2011).
8 Daniel Kahneman, *Thinking Fast and Slow* (Penguin, 2011).
9 Information on cognitive biases can be found in a number of places. We found the following valuable:
   https://openpolicy.blog.gov.uk/2018/08/13/bias-busters-who-you-gonna-call/
   www.weforum.org/agenda/2021/11/humans-cognitive-bias-mistake/
   www.ncbi.nlm.nih.gov/pmc/articles/PMC10071311/
10 www.palacios-huerta.com/docs/professionals.pdf
11 Daniel Kahneman, *Thinking Fast and Slow* (Penguin, 2011), p. 250.
12 This is the idea based on crime management, popularised by Kelling and Wilson in 1982, that in order to reduce crime it is important to focus on minor infractions as ignoring those creates a more permissive environment for major infractions. See www.theatlantic.com/magazine/archive/1982/03/broken-windows/304465/
13 The 1854 report by Stafford Northcote and Charles Trevelyan laid the foundations for an impartial civil service, where entry and promotion would be based on merit, not political favour, www.civilservant.org.uk/library/1854_Northcote_Trevelyan_Report.pdf
14 https://assets.publishing.service.gov.uk/government/uploads/system/uploads/attachment_data/file/1171616/Department_for_Education_Consolidated_annual_report_and_accounts_2023.pdf
15 www.bbc.co.uk/news/uk-politics-66174373
16 www.ft.com/content/0f88b52b-dc94-4ef0-a6b7-ffe6bf6fdc7d
17 www.theguardian.com/politics/2020/aug/26/top-dfe-civil-servant-jonathan-slater-to-step-down-after-exams-row
18 https://schoolsweek.co.uk/daniel-kebede-elected-as-neu-general-secretary/
19 https://schoolsweek.co.uk/patrick-roach-elected-unopposed-as-nasuwt-general-secretary/

20 https://assets.publishing.service.gov.uk/government/uploads/system/uploads/atta chment_data/file/662767/LA_expenditure_Childrens_Services_Update.pdf
21 www.gov.uk/government/publications/2010-to-2015-government-policy-looked-a fter-children-and-adoption/2010-to-2015-government-policy-looked-after-children-a nd-adoption
22 https://assets.publishing.service.gov.uk/government/uploads/system/uploads/atta chment_data/file/535043/Childrens_services_spending_delivery_report_Aldaba_EIF_ July_2016.pdf
23 www.publicfirst.co.uk/public-first-research-finds-parental-support-for-fulltime-schooling-ha s-collapsed.html
24 www.bbc.co.uk/news/uk-politics-64803947
25 www.gov.uk/government/news/thousands-more-pupils-to-receive-support-to-impr ove-attendance

2 How do organisational histories and dynamics shape decisions?

On 10 July 2023, a reception was held to mark the imminent retirement of Mary Bousted and Kevin Courtney as joint General Secretaries of the NEU. It may have surprised some that Nick Gibb spoke – Minister of State for School Standards at the time and an often-fearsome critic of the NEU. In his remarks it is reported he said, 'We agree on almost nothing...but we are committed to the same outcomes...it's been a pleasure working with you both.'[1] Against the backdrop of teacher strikes and habitually divisive rhetoric from both government and unions, Minister Gibb's comments nonetheless reflect the fact that there are both personal and organisational dynamics at play when deciding policy.

There is an acceptance – at least in public and even amongst bitter rivals in the system – that there is a shared commitment to similar outcomes. In other words, it is not necessarily what we are all trying to achieve that provokes disagreement but the way different people want to achieve it. Things very quickly break down beyond generic statements of intent. We are unable to even agree definitively on what we mean by 'good' in terms of teachers or schools for example – or indeed outcomes – so it is no surprise that there are so many views on what policies should be pursued.

In the previous chapter we described the formative and responsive forces at play that all involved in education policy-making and delivery have to navigate as they confront the circumstances of their own position and responsibilities. Perhaps the most important contexts are the organisations they find themselves operating within, all of which have their own cultures and histories which shape the responses they give. It is remarkable how often the change in a Secretary of State, or even a change of government, can feel largely seamless to those working in schools, and there is a continuity of instinct and action that belies the influence of individual decision-making.

Put another way, the respect between Nick Gibb and Mary Bousted seems genuine. As far as we can tell, they seem to actually like one another on a personal level. You would think that this would be a solid basis for conversation and negotiation, even in policy areas about which they may have disagreed vehemently. The reason that these personal relationships – and indeed the personalities of the people involved more widely – are limited in their impact is because of the organisations they work for. Nick Gibb was a longstanding minister in a

DOI: 10.4324/9781032651057-3

Conservative Government; Mary Bousted the joint General Secretary of a teaching union. These organisational contexts – driven by their histories – did more to shape the relationship between the two than any personal or intellectual positions.

That is why, in this chapter, we will look at the broader historical trends that have shaped organisational positions, and look at the individual organisational cultures and incentives that constrain the impact of individual views and ideas.

A brief history of education in England

The history of public education in England stems back well over 150 years, and builds on millennia of private and church-led education that has helped to create some of the oldest and best-known institutions of education in the world. It is notable that the history of government intervention in education is different to other areas of public policy. The general view of successive Victorian governments was that the role of the state was in providing a framework for voluntary sector organisations (church schools, charitable hospitals, etc.) to operate. Unlike in health – where government focused on specific issues related to the wider public wellbeing (sanitation, pollution, etc.) – in education the government was interested in the results of investment. The government provided grants to schools to try to improve the education level of the populace (like today, justified in terms of helping to ensure Britain's economic advantage in the world), before passing the 1870 Elementary Education Act,[2] which established local school boards (funded by local taxes) to oversee the delivery of education for children up to the age of 12. It represents the first attempt to create a national framework for the delivery of education in England, and the impact was dramatic with huge growth in both the number of pupils attending schools and the number of teachers working in them. The reach of government was extended by the 1902 Balfour Act, which gave local authorities the powers previously held by local school boards and stretched their influence into secondary as well as elementary education. And in the 1918 Fisher Education Act,[3] fees for elementary education were abolished and the school leaving age was set at 14 – universal, free education was now to be a reality across the country.

In comparison, in the health sector the government focused in the 1875 Public Health Act on creating duties for local councils to improve sewage and sanitation. It was not until the 1919 Ministry of Health Act that the government created a national infrastructure to oversee the provision of health care, and of course in 1945 the NHS was born.

In other words, for many decades, in education the government became involved directly in the provision, whereas in health it focused on the wider issues causing ill health rather than the provision of medical care. This had a profound impact on the way in which organisations working with government formed in these two sectors.

In education, it meant that from the mid-nineteenth century, unions and their predecessors were involved directly with the government in agreeing what the very notion of education should be. Successive governments were motivated to focus on the success of what went on in the classroom, basing much of their funding on 'payment by results' – from 1839 to 1897 grants to elementary schools depended on a satisfactory report by an inspector (the birth of His Majesty's Inspector) that the school was meeting minimum standards of quality of education and pupil attendance. So unions, working on behalf of their members, were immediately drawn into conversations about the quality of teaching – indeed, the entire premise of education – not just the terms of conditions of their members.

In contrast, those working in the health sector did not have to contend with government interest in terms of what happened in the consulting room or the operating theatre. In this context, union-type organisations such as the British Medical Association and its predecessors were able to focus on issues such as regulation of the profession and sharing scientific knowledge, working with a more sophisticated network of specialist Royal Colleges and Deaneries, many of which had histories stretching back before the Enlightenment. It is notable that the Chartered College of Teaching (and its predecessors the College of Teachers and the College of Preceptors) has hitherto had nothing like the same level of influence over the practice of the profession.

As well as the broader point, the specific history of how different education unions have risen and fallen matters. In 1880, when 180 women who worked in schools for educating girls met to form the Association of Assistant Mistresses (AAM), they were mostly focused on the pupils. In 1891, the Association of Assistant Masters in Secondary School was set up to protect and improve conditions of service. In 1879, the National Union of Elementary Teachers (NUET) fought to protect a teacher accused of obtaining exam papers and passing them on to his pupils.[4] Early campaigns were fought against payment by results, and the National Union of Teachers (NUT, as the NUET became) dealt with both national policy-making with the Board of Education and with the employer at school or local level.[5] As Michael Barber points out, much of the early work of the unions was around pay, conditions of service and entry to the profession – employment issues. These included campaigns against 'extraneous duties' including 'being required to play the organ in church on Sunday'.[6] However, because its stated aim was to establish 'a teaching profession on a par with doctors', the NUT's work was broader than individual pay and conditions, focusing on the control of entry into the profession and control of its own inspection. This meant, by necessity, adopting a range of methods to influence Parliament and politicians, including organising delegations to meet with constituency MPs, briefing allies in Parliament, and canvassing candidates at election times. They kept registers of promises made by MPs, and in 1877 resolved to support members to be elected to Parliament.

As teachers became more organised through the unions, their social status improved, and it became increasingly possible for them to have more influence over education policy. At the same time, that influence was leavened by splits within the education union movement, some of which are still felt in rivalries that persist today. It is, for example, still relevant to understand the historical shifts that led the National Association of Schoolmasters (NAS – originally the National Association of Men Teachers, but it quickly changed its name in 1920) to form as a separate organisation within and then outside the NUT after the First World War (largely to protect the rights of male teachers who, when returning from war, found many of their jobs taken by female teachers demanding equal pay), and to understand how the merger with the Union of Women Teachers (with its own complicated history) came about in 1976. These historical legacies retain power through a general culture of distrust and competitiveness between the two main unions for classroom teachers.

The formation of separate unions for school leaders was motivated in part by the need to create a separate bargaining position with the government for headteachers. The NAHT was formed in 1897 (as the London Head Teachers Association) to offer a different perspective when presenting ideas to politicians,[7] not least to draw a distinction between the perceived professionalism and high social standing of headteachers compared to classroom teachers. The Association of School and College Leaders (ASCL)[8] has a similarly lengthy lineage as the descendant of the Association of Headmistresses (AHM, formed 1874) and the Headmasters Association (HMA, formed 1890). This split between leadership and classroom teachers reflects the fact that teachers campaigning for employment rights were generally set against the headteachers who were charged with running the school, including managing budgets and making salary decisions.

The post-war settlement in education

After 1945, very different relationships developed between government and the education and health sectors. The NHS created a national, funded infrastructure for the provision of health care, and there were plenty of doctors who did not like being 'nationalised', not least in terms of the impact on their salaries. It took the government into conversations about administration, building, organisation, recruitment, salaries, relationships between different medical professions, but not directly into the delivery of medical advice and procedures. In fact, throughout its history, the NHS has never had to contend with a Minister for Health intervening in the specifics of medical provision in the way that governments of all persuasions have become much more present in the classroom, directing teachers in a way that doctors and nurses do not have to contend with.

The increasing level of government involvement in the practice of teaching has been gradual but consistent. In the initial post-war period, education policy was dominated by the 1944 Butler Act, which provided for free education up to the age of 15 through the 'tripartite' approach of grammar, technical, and secondary modern schools, and the need to build up the number of teachers. Government took on the role of providing funding to the system, but did not engage in the detail of what took place within those schools. Instead, government focused on creating the infrastructure and fabric for the new system – in particular through recruitment of more teachers and the building of schools.

Most children did not progress onto O levels, let alone A levels. The purpose of education was more closely linked to the need to provide a smaller educated class to oversee the larger labouring class still employed in industry. There was no national curriculum. In fact, according to Derek Gillard in his comprehensive history of education in the UK,[9] the 1944 Act does not use the word 'curriculum' at all, and the minister, RA Butler (often known as RAB Butler), told the House of Commons in the debates on the bill:

> It has been felt that, in certain areas, there is a danger that the Secretary, or director of education, may fancy himself in certain subjects, or in some branch of study, and may go into a school and, by an obiter dictum, try to direct the secular instruction of that school more, as he would say, according to the wishes of the authority. That sort of interference with the individual life of the school is undesirable.[10]

This framing by Butler shaped the relationship with the teaching unions for the next 15–20 years, during which time the focus was on expanding membership (as more teachers were recruited) and negotiating on terms and conditions as Britain grew following the ravages of the war. There was little need for unions to be defensive about any government attempts to interfere with what happened in the classroom.

The secret garden

This balance started to shift in the 1960s, in part because of wider structural changes in the British economy as well as the evolution of social views on class, aspiration, and identity. Britain was becoming a different place and the heavy industry of the past – which was powered by a large pool of labour that did not need any significant secondary education – was under threat from global economic changes that drove successive governments to seek to keep children in school longer and educate them more. Higher education in particular underwent a seismic change as new universities were built and the number going into higher education rose from 3.4% in 1950, 8.4% in 1970, 19.3% in 1990, and 33% in 2000.[11] As the post-war recovery period gave way to the optimistic change of the 1960s and the geopolitical challenges of the 1970s, government changed its attitude to education policy, becoming more inclined to intervene in the world traditionally reserved for unions and the teaching profession.

This change, can be seen in a speech by David Eccles to the House of Commons in March 1960 when he promised to 'sally into the secret garden of the curriculum':

> We hardly ever discuss what is taught to the 7 million boys and girls in the maintained schools ... Of course, Parliament would never attempt to dictate the curriculum, but, from time to time, we could with advantage express views on what is taught in schools and in training colleges.[12]

The then Labour Party leader, Harold Wilson, in his famous 1963 'white heat' speech to the Labour conference,[13] showed how his future government would look to transform society to respond to the modern challenges facing Britain. The emerging consensus across both parties in the 1960s was around a fuller role for government to play in what happened in classrooms.

The position was very different from the perspective of the unions. As the government began to become more closely involved in decisions about the curriculum, the NUT in particular set up in opposition to ministerial influence. This divergence is in part captured in the different responses to the influential 1967 Plowden Report. This was a review of primary education commissioned in 1963 (under a Conservative Government) that was led by Baroness Plowden, reporting to the Labour Government in power in 1967. The report ran to nearly 200 recommendations,[14] and for the members of teaching unions those focusing on a 'child-centred' approach seemed to capture a modern mood to move away from more traditional methods of education, methods and approaches that had been demonstrated in Plowden's work as tending to fail those children in poorer areas (described as Educational Priority Areas). The educational psychological approach embodied in Plowden forms the basis of what is now (often pejoratively) referred to as the progressive approach to teaching,[15] and it drew an immediate and negative response from some, espoused most fully in the so-called 'Black Papers' circulated between 1969–77,[16] intended to offer an alternative to government White Papers. As Angus Maude said in the first Black Paper:

> Taking a long view, one must conclude that the most serious danger facing Britain is the threat to the quality of education at all levels. The motive force behind this threat is the ideology of egalitarianism.[17]

As the 1960s rolled into the 1970s, ministers continued to be cautious and publicly supported the work of Plowden even if implementing the recommendations sparingly. It is noteworthy however that the body that led the production of the Plowden Report – the Central Advisory Council for Education (CACE) – formed as part of the 1944 Butler Act and dominated by teachers – was never asked to oversee work for the government again and was ultimately disbanded.

The catalyst for government action was the William Tynedale affair in 1974–75.[18] The William Tynedale Junior School, in Islington, implemented what it felt was – and which was presented as – a thoroughly progressive approach to education. This included a fiercely 'child-centred' approach with little effort to create discipline from teachers nor to bring parents on board with more radical approaches. In what could be seen clearly as at best a misplaced interpretation of Plowden's work, teachers began to ignore pupils who they did not deem were disadvantaged.[19]

The William Tynedale affair did not create opposition to progressive methods – they existed in the 'Black Papers' and elsewhere – but the significant publicity – including in the national press as the affair played out – was catnip to those intent on reasserting more traditional approaches to education, and gave government the impetus it needed to intervene more forcefully in what was taught in schools and how it was taught. In his famous 1976 Ruskin Speech, then Prime Minister James Callaghan proposed that very little in education should be off limits for politicians to debate:

Public interest is strong and legitimate and will be satisfied. We spend £6bn a year on education, so there will be discussion. ... Let me repeat some of the fields that need study because they cause concern. There are the methods and aims of informal instruction, the strong case for the so-called 'core curriculum' of basic knowledge; next, what is the proper way of monitoring the use of resources in order to maintain a proper national standard of performance; then there is the role of the inspectorate in relation to national standards; and there is the need to improve relations between industry and education.[20]

Although Callaghan was clear that his government – through his Secretary of State Shirley Williams – would be taking a new interest in these areas, he was still committed to working with the system, including unions, teachers, and parents. But whether Callaghan intended it or not,[21] the prevailing wisdom of educational thinking tended towards greater levels of government control, more centralisation, and more intervention.

We can see this in the 1988 Education Reform Act, which saw a Conservative Government bring in the national curriculum, setting out what should be taught and introducing a key stage structure to schools, along with key stage testing which both made sure the new curriculum was being taught and paved the way for national, local, and school-by-school comparisons of outcomes. We can see it in the creation of Ofsted in 1992, and its continued support by every subsequent government. We can see it in the policies of the Labour Government from 1997 as it developed the literacy and numeracy strategies, later combined to become the National Strategies, which set out in detail how teachers should teach those subjects, introducing 'the three-part lesson' and 'the plenary'. And we can see it in multiple reforms of initial teacher training (from the end of non-graduate teaching routes after 1979 through to the introduction of the Early Career Framework in 2019). From the mid-1970s onwards, subsequent governments have become more and more closely involved in the day-to-day business of the classroom.

The position of teaching unions has, throughout this period, been largely one of opposition. From the Ruskin speech onwards, the NUT has opposed successive attempts by the government to intervene in what happens in the classroom, which is not surprising given the history of unions in education as set out above. What is more surprising is the union criticism of attempts to undo some of these reforms since 2010. For example, the national curriculum was forcefully opposed by unions as it was being conceived, subject to intense attack as it was being rolled out, and then constantly questioned as it has been delivered. As part of a 2009 inquiry by the Children and Families Select Committee (the previous name of the now Education Select Committee), the NUT submitted evidence noting this engagement:

Prior to the 1988 Education Reform Act, it is fair to say that the NUT was opposed to the idea of any nationally prescribed curriculum but the intense debate created by the 1988 Act hot-housed the Union's thinking about what a curriculum should be for.[22]

As part of the same evidence, the NUT called for greater flexibility in the implementation of the national curriculum:

> Teachers who are treated as professionals and who have the confidence and skills to make professional judgements based on research, evidence and experience are well placed to manage and influence a flexible curriculum ... The DCSF[23] and the Government must ensure that teachers are given back this freedom and confidence in order for the personalisation agenda to work effectively for all children and young people.[24]

Yet when, after 2010, Michael Gove expanded the academies programme, dramatically increasing the number of schools no longer legally required to teach the national curriculum, the NUT opposed this move as creating an insupportable inconsistency in the delivery of education.

The question begs itself: are unions, historically speaking, motivated more by substance or the principle of opposition? And, to offer the question from the other side: is the government, historically speaking, motivated more by control or by bettering outcomes for students?

How history shapes the present: the formation of modern organisational cultures

As we can see from a brief historical survey, government and education unions have been interested in what happens in the classroom in a way that is very different in, say, the health sector. When viewed in the longer term, the period of post-war consensus – during which government remained aloof from curriculum and teaching methods and unions adhered to traditional methods of teaching – was in some ways an anomaly. Competition and disagreement has been the more common prevailing relationship, and this fact still shapes the way in which both government and unions operate today. We argue that has been the more common order of things within the English education system based on the historical legacy of the organisations involved in policy-making.

This is an important fact to bear in mind whenever there is a call for the depoliticisation of education – the undeniably attractive idea that there is some evidence-based education policy nirvana that we could reach if only vested interest was taken out of the equation – that we should all just find a way to 'let teachers teach'. As the William Tynedale affair shows, there is always a case to balance the wishes of educationalists and parents, and the funding and engagement of the state rests on a political basis.

We want to suggest that there are three main ways in which the organisational cultures of the major players in the education system are able to constrain – even override – the individual wishes of key decision-makers: through institutional memory, policy networks, and mutually beneficial antagonism.

Institutional memory

One explanation for the continuity of approaches in different organisations is institutional memory – the collection of knowledge that accrues over time that is held within an organisation and shapes current thinking (consciously or otherwise). Christopher Pollitt describes this as taking four forms of 'organisational memory':

- The experience and knowledge of the existing staff: what is 'in their heads';
- The technical systems, including electronic databases and various kinds of paper records;
- The management system (organizational routines and standard operating procedures commonly build in knowledge acquired from previous operating experiences);
- The norms and values of the organizational culture. These can function as a sort of memory – certainly as an element of continuity: 'this is the way we do things around here'.[25]

Although often viewed through the lens of the civil service – as it is the state bureaucracy – these forms of institutional memory are present in every organisation, including unions, businesses, academia, and schools. Pollitt considers the civil service and argues that each of these forms has been eroded over the years.

We can start with high staff turnover, and we have already noted how most civil servants are not experts in the area they lead, even if they are career civil servants. The same is generally true for ministers, and even those who do hang around have to deal with an ever-changing landscape. For example, Nick Gibb was a Schools Minister (with various titles) on and off since 2010, but he was fired twice and subject to reshuffle rumours many more times. He served as a minister under six different Secretaries of State, each with different priorities (and remarkably missed the tenures of four more in the little more than a year he was on the backbenches between September 2021 and October 2022), and was part of many more ministerial teams (at least 27 other people have served as ministers at the Department for Education since 2010[26]). The officials supporting him changed numerous times (he worked with four Permanent Secretaries, not including interim appointments, and had literally hundreds, if not thousands, of changes of officials across all levels). This demonstrates two things – first, that Nick Gibb had to navigate significant change in the organisation he was a fixture of and, second, that he is very much the exception that proves the rule.

Around shifting ministers, civil servants, and other policy-makers, the government has implemented a variety of new electronic filing systems, not always driven by the desire to make information easily shareable and accessible. Ways of operating have shifted, breaking down some of the organisational approaches previously common. And organisational culture is never a static thing. Pollitt suggests that this is new for the civil service, and that there was a point when these forms used to be more solid in the civil service (something others dispute[27]), and moreover that such forms are conducive to good policy-making, again something that Grube and others suggest is not possible or desirable to pursue as an ideal.[28]

That things have changed is undeniable. What would an official joining the then Department for Education and Skills have found 20 years ago?[29] Files were still largely in hard copy, with extensive filing cabinets around the office floor in Sanctuary Buildings and a large external file storage site near Sheffield. To get those files Wales Bar (the storage site) needed to be contacted and the file would be couriered down. Most files were open to all, but some had more restrictive access. The hierarchy of the organisation was apparent in the fabric of the building. The floors had been made open plan only recently, and only for staff below Grade 7. Those Grade 7 and above had their own offices, the size of which was determined by your grade. Junior officials seldom got to spend time with ministers or the most senior officials, instead having to brief team leaders to prepare them for the occasion, and these meetings were always face-to-face – no minister used 'teleconferencing' as it was then known. Submissions and briefings were now produced on a computer, but were still printed out and given to a superior to comment on in hard copy, sometimes passed around to anybody who might need to comment so that the returning copy would be covered in multiple scrawls of varying legibility for the original author to decode and reconcile. Submissions had to be taken in hard copy to ministers' offices with all annexes flagged, given to their private secretary to read, comment on, and put in the box. Sanctuary Buildings had an on-site library with a range of relevant texts and legislation, supported by a librarian. Most teams had administrators as part of them, with jobs like fetching the post or sharing relevant sections from that week's Hansard.

This may seem like a bygone era to many new civil servants and nobody can deny that the growth of technology has transformed how information is shared, briefings are produced, and ministers are engaged. Electronic red boxes, WhatsApp exchanges with officials into the evening, and everybody (bar ministers) in the open-plan office space means that the department feels like a different place in lots of ways. The library is, alas, long gone. Does this all mean that institutional memory has disappeared?

The short answer is no. The structures of government – and in particular the Department for Education in this context – ensure that a significant portion of institutional memory is retained. Although the officials may change and team titles shift with the fashions of the time, the areas that the department is responsible for are based on legislation, guidance, and funding relationships that are complicated to unpick. When the next Secretary of State arrives at Sanctuary Buildings, they will be confronted with briefing from all bits of their new realm about areas of policy about which they may have had little capacity to engage with meaningfully before, but will nonetheless demand their attention. Policy teams that exist now have existed in various forms for decades and carry within them their own sort of inertia because they have been dealing with the same issues for many years.

In fact, you could argue that institutional memory is perhaps too strong given the repetition of previous ideas over many decades – see Plowden's recommendation to create Education Priority Areas in 1967, David Blunkett creating Education Action Zones in 1998,[30] or even the 2022 Schools White Paper, which set out plans for new Priority Education Investment Areas. For places like Liverpool which were designated in all three of these versions of area-based support, the interest of the Department for Education must feel tenacious indeed!

For some this repetition may feel indicative of a stifling culture that leads to an expectation on how things are done that can limit creativity and progression, at worst emblematic of a sclerotic decline that organisations are unable to break free from; the rhythms of the civil service feel inevitable and, although it may not learn, it does not forget. In fact, rather than suggest that the high turnover of staff erodes institutional memory, we would argue that it can enhance it because it takes a significant amount of knowledge and effort to make major changes to the education system, and these rely on longevity and political will. In the absence of security of tenure or expertise, a kind of inertia exerts itself. Ideas are reinvented, policy positions ebb and flow, and not enough actually changes. Unions tend to have much greater longevity at the top,[31] but are still subject to the same sense of inertia, suggesting that any focus on individuals is largely unproductive.

Without wanting to overcook an idea, we might choose to look at this institutional memory as a form of unconscious bias at an organisational level, the way an institution operates automatically without an effortful thought to do something different. System 1 overruling system 2 (in the terms of Kahneman).

Policy networks

Another way in which historical influences shape the way organisations operate is in the networks within which ideas are formed and promoted. This is something of a self-fulfilling process as the more a network attracts particular types of thinking, the more that type of thinking is represented in the network and becomes refined and promoted. Moreover, by creating networks focused on particular ways of thinking, a narrower 'consensus' is formed within those networks that tends to promote their ideas as right, selecting facts and views that suit a purpose.

We can demonstrate this by looking at Minister Nick Gibb's evidence to a Lord's Committee:

> As I said, when we conducted the curriculum review we appointed Tim Oates, an assessment expert, to chair it. We took evidence and consulted. Even once we had produced drafts in all the curriculum areas, we consulted widely. The notion that it was Michael Gove and I who sat down one night with a glass of wine and a biro and wrote it is just nonsense. We took expert evidence, including from around the world.[32]

Policy-making has always drawn on expertise and on a range of different people and organisations, but if we think about this for a moment we will see it is not as straightforward as Gibb wants to make out. The national curriculum review was carried out in large part by a small team of experts appointed by Gove. One of those was Tim Oates, a researcher whose 'pen portrait' makes clear that he had 'advised the UK Government for many years on both practical matters and assessment policy and is particularly experienced in international use of core knowledge curricula'.[33] The other three had considerable academic and teaching expertise across curriculum and assessment in both primary and secondary schools.

They were given a detailed remit, setting out an expectation that they would 'draw on a robust evidence base ..., taking account of the requirements set by successful education jurisdictions across the world',[34] as well as seeking and reflecting the views of teachers and others. They were required to make recommendations on, amongst other things:

- the essential knowledge (e.g. facts, concepts, principles and fundamental operations) that children need to be taught ...
- the extent to which the content of the National Curriculum should be set out on a year by year basis in order to ensure that essential knowledge is built systematically and consistently.[35]

They were told that the national curriculum should contain English, mathematics, science, and physical education, and were asked whether any others, from a list of eight subjects, should also have statutory Programmes of Study. So, while it was true to say that the government set up an Expert Panel to review the national curriculum – even framing the work as an effort to reduce prescription in the 2010 White Paper, *The Importance of Teaching*, [36] it also set very clear parameters about the sort of curriculum it expected to see, many of which would be welcome to those who had drafted the Black Papers 40 years earlier.

Of course, Nick Gibb did not remind the Committee that the Expert Panel disagreed publicly on the recommendations that were drawn up. In an excoriating blog post,[37] Professor Andrew Pollard, one of the four members of the panel, suggested that the process was flawed from the start. In his view, the voice that was most influential in the development of the curriculum did not come from the wealth of evidence collected in previous reviews, nor the views and expertise of the teachers and others who contributed to this one. Instead, the influence came from the American E.D. Hirsch, of whom Nick Gibb was a huge fan. Hirsch had collated a 'core knowledge sequence' for every year group from preschool to Grade 8 (age 13–14). So, rather than taking an open view of the world's best curricula, the outcome was largely pre-determined by government and a panel was convened who would either agree with that outcome or be disregarded. The Expert Panel recommended that the Programmes of Study be organised on a two-year basis, but it was the Hirsch model of detailed content year on year that won the day. Three of the four members of the Expert Panel resigned, leaving the chair, Tim Oates, to work with ministers and the Department for Education to develop the Programmes of Study.

All governments rely on their chosen experts to develop advice. People become the experts of choice through a variety of routes, many because of their headship of successful schools, schools which have been 'turned around' and moved from 'inadequate' to 'outstanding'. Others have developed expertise in assessment and curriculum, through exam boards and agencies, or as academics. Some may advise from a position in the House of Lords, having been ministers or leaders of unions or charities. Our intention here is not to dispute the expertise of any of these, nor to suggest that consulting with experts is the wrong thing for governments to do. The problem is that these experts can be drawn from quite a small group, so that often the same names crop up repeatedly. For example, Tim Oates is still often involved, most recently as part of a group advising the Prime Minister on Maths to 18. Many begin their expert journeys as headteachers selected for advisory panels, gradually becoming more influential. Some, such as the former head of Mossbourne Academy, take on greater roles such as His Majesty's Chief Inspector of Schools. Others move through a range of groups and panels, advising on a variety of different educational and other issues, for example Katharine Birbalsingh, a headteacher who became, briefly, chair of the Social Mobility Commission.

If we allow experts to be hand-picked, the outcome is inevitably a sort of intergenerational groupthink, as historical trends and ideas become reinforcing within a political party, a union, a group of like-minded people who seek one another out year after year and bolster already held biases and notions.

Mutually beneficial antagonism

As it currently stands, too many policy ideas are shaped by inertia and bias rather than need and evidence. An idea is formed and pursued, with evidence found post hoc to justify rather than enlighten. Institutional memory leads to repetition rather than wisdom and those in power tend to surround themselves with comforting networks rather than those providing constructive challenge.

Such an approach is hardly likely to inspire confidence, so why does it continue? The short answer is that the organisational dynamics in the system operate in a confrontational fashion in which different ideas and perspectives elide into entrenched positions and grandstanding arguments that do little to advance the policy debate but which provide a rallying cry for people to gather around.

Government needs to find someone or something to blame for issues as a way of getting leverage to justify policies, whether that be the policies of the opposition party, the pernicious influence of 'The Blob', or extraneous factors such as the global economy or geopolitical situation. Unions need to create opposition with the government to generate interest amongst members for action, or amongst one another to provide reasons for teachers to move between unions. This means that, as noted previously, they have been vehemently opposed to the introduction of a national curriculum and aghast at the idea that any school could be allowed not to follow the national curriculum, for example. Lobby groups must make their issue one of major concern in order to get policy-makers involved.

Unions are set up to protect and to represent their members. In order to be heard, to wield any power in negotiations, it helps to have a large membership. In order to have a large membership in a sector which has a number of unions, sometimes unions need to exaggerate differences between their policy positions or values, often drawing on the long history of separation outlined above. These differences may be genuine but often the competition is less about differences of position and more about 'going it alone'. For a period in the 2010s, the

NASUWT refused to take part in collaborative activity with the other unions, even when the work that was being done was the same. While the other unions published pay scales and guidance jointly as teacher and headteacher unions, NASUWT published its own that was almost identical. Later, NUT and NASUWT joined together in a partnership around workload which included joint guidance and support for industrial action in schools, while the ATL developed its own workload campaign. For a long time, there was competition between the NUT and the NASUWT around membership numbers, with each claiming that they were the largest. And then the NUT and ATL went one further and merged to become the NEU, leading the NASUWT to play up their position as 'the Teachers' Union'. Even as recently as the 2023 Party Conference season, NASUWT were hosting fringe events themselves, while the NEU, ASCL, and NAHT worked together on events. These differences mean that it is much too easy for the government to pick and choose which unions to work with, and they also make it very difficult for the unions themselves to sit down together and come up with solutions to the issues at hand.

Sometimes conflicts amount to political positioning. Union members come from all political positions and none, but the union movement is traditionally left wing. Those who become influential in the union movement are often further to the left than their membership, which tends to drag any public position into opposition to power structures, i.e. government. This makes it easier for the government to characterise the union movement as regressive, being able to focus on the more presentationally challenging areas of union work rather than the substance behind different strands of thinking. Ironically, unions are only allowed to ballot for strike action on issues of terms and conditions – not policy – and yet it suits both unions and government to characterise strike action as much broader, quickly framing any action in moral terms (as either defending or damaging children).

This level of conflict has increasingly pervaded the whole system, reaching schools that feel the competitive pressure of Ofsted outcomes, exam results, league tables (even if unofficially produced by local papers), and so on. Some may posit the theory that competition drives up performance, and there may be some truth to that in specific circumstances, but it comes at the cost of the wider system. For example, a school with a strong track record finds it easier to recruit teachers, whereas one on a journey of improvement is likely to find that more difficult, as demonstrated by a report into so-called 'stuck schools' undertaken by the Education Policy Institute and UCL's Institute of Education.[38] In this 2022 study, 580 stuck schools (defined as schools that had achieved an overall Ofsted rating below 'good' for three inspections undertaken between 2005 and 2018) had a significantly higher turnover of staff (73% in primary and 72% in secondary, compared to 54% in non-stuck primaries and 56% in non-stuck secondaries). Stuck schools also had higher rates of free school meals, pupils living in poor neighbourhoods, and higher rates of SEND. In other words, stuck schools had pupils with greater needs but suffered from a much higher turnover of staff, which can only be deleterious to pupil learning.

These findings are backed up by a 2021 study undertaken on behalf of the UK Office of Manpower Economics,[39] which asked teachers how long they intended to stay at their current school, broken down by Ofsted inspection grade. In 'Outstanding' schools, 29% said they expected to stay for less than two years. This rose to 53% in 'Inadequate' schools. In comparison just 7% of teachers in 'Inadequate' schools thought they would be there five years later, compared to 22% in 'Outstanding' schools.

The point here is not directly about Ofsted but rather the way it works within a system to create competitive judgements that have a direct and negative impact on behaviour, with teachers seeking to leave the challenging schools when those are the schools – or more particularly the pupils – most likely to benefit from consistency.

Almost since it was introduced, in 1992, the relationship between Ofsted and teachers, and their unions, has been a difficult one. Perhaps the most well known of Chief Inspectors, Chris Woodhead, famously began his role by claiming there were '15,000 incompetent teachers',[40] while promising to root out 'mediocrity, failure and complacency'. Later, Sir Michael Wilshaw, as Chief Inspector, is reported to have said to headteachers: 'If anyone says to you that: "staff morale is at an all-time low" you know you are doing something right.'[41] Both have suggested that they have had to 'battle' the unions in order to improve schools. So while Ofsted, and government, will point to evidence of schools improving, with increasing numbers being 'outstanding' and fewer graded as 'requires improvement', as well as data from parent surveys about how useful Ofsted reports are for choosing schools, unions cite evidence from teachers about the impact of inspections on their workload and morale, evidence from previous inspection frameworks of the different judgements made in different parts of the country, and the lack of evidence from Ofsted of its own inspectors' reliability.

This reflects a truth that acts on all organisations – there is short-term gain to be found in opposition and antagonism. There are also internal organisational pressures that prevent those who might try to seek compromise or common ground. These are unhelpful when it comes to thinking about creating a better way of policy-making in the future.

Chapter summary

- There is a genuine desire amongst most involved in education policy-making to create a better environment for children to learn, but there is little agreement on how to achieve it.
- This is in part because of the histories of and dynamics between different organisations involved that channel policy-makers down different paths.
- Historically, education is an area with significant government intervention, including what happens in the classroom, meaning that unions were formed to focus on policy ideas as well as terms and conditions.
- After a brief post-war period of consolidation, the education debate from the 1960s onwards entrenched the debate amongst 'traditionalists' and 'progressives' that still exists today.

- This debate colours institutional memory, which is pervasive but not creative.
- It also shapes the networks from which policy-makers draw ideas and seek to implement them.
- In the absence of genuine learning and challenge, we instead have a destructive cycle of mutually beneficial antagonism baked into the organisational dynamics governing policy-making and implementation.

Notes

1 https://twitter.com/FCDWhittaker/status/1678482065652609031
2 www.parliament.uk/about/living-heritage/transformingsociety/livinglearning/school/overview/1870educationact/
3 The Fisher Education Act was also the first time government legislated to keep children in some form of education until the age of 18. Despite multiple attempts it would take until 2015 for the reality to come to pass (based on the 2008 Education and Skills Act).
4 www.tes.com/magazine/archive/100-years-unions
5 Michael Barber, *Education and the Teacher Unions* (Continuum, 1992), p. 3.
6 Ibid., p.5.
7 www.naht.org.uk/About-Us/Our-history
8 www.ascl.org.uk/About-us/Who-we-are/History-of-ASCL. The AHM and HMA merged in 1977 to create the Secondary Heads Association, and in 2006 became the Association of School and College Leaders to recognise a wider membership base.
9 Derek Gillard, *Education in the UK: A History* (2018), www.education-uk.org/history
10 *Hansard*, House of Commons, 10 March 1944, Vol. 397, Cols 2363–4.
11 https://researchbriefings.files.parliament.uk/documents/SN04252/SN04252.pdf
12 https://api.parliament.uk/historic-hansard/commons/1960/mar/21/education-report-of-the-central-advisory
13 https://web-archives.univ-pau.fr/english/TD2doc2.pdf
14 https://education-uk.org/documents/plowden/
15 https://education-uk.org/documents/plowden/plowdenore-01.html
16 www.jstor.org/stable/41553758
17 Taken from the first Black Paper, *Critical Survey*, Volume 4, Number 1, written by Angus Maude. www.jstor.org/stable/41553759
18 www.jstor.org/stable/1050913
19 Ibid.
20 https://education-uk.org/documents/speeches/1976ruskin.html
21 Silverwood and Wolstencraft argue that post-hoc misinterpretation of the Ruskin speech has been used widely to justify policies that Callaghan would not have promoted, https://bera-journals.onlinelibrary.wiley.com/doi/10.1002/berj.3868
22 https://publications.parliament.uk/pa/cm200809/cmselect/cmchilsch/344/8061106.htm
23 DCSF – the Department for Children, Schools and Families, between 2007 and 2010 a previous name and version of the current Department for Education.
24 https://publications.parliament.uk/pa/cm200809/cmselect/cmchilsch/344/8061106.htm
25 https://onlinelibrary.wiley.com/doi/full/10.1111/j.1467-9299.2008.01738.x
26 In no particular order, ministers at the Department for Education include: Robin Walker, Will Quince, Jonathan Gullis, Robert Halfon, Andrea Jenkins, Alex Burghart, Claire Coutinho, Tim Loughton, Edward Timpson, Robert Goodwill, Kemi Badenoch, Vicky Ford, David Johnston, Brendan Clark-Smith, Kelly Tolhurst, Baroness Barran, Baroness Berridge, Lord Agnew, Lord Nash, Lord Hill, Sarah Teather, Liz Truss, David Laws, Matt Hancock, Jo Johnson, Anne Milton, and Nick Boles. In addition,

Nadim Zahawi, Gillian Keegan, and Michelle Donelan were ministers at the Department before they were Secretaries of State. Caroline Dinage was notionally at the Department as well, but covered the Women and Equalities brief.
27 Denis Grube suggests both that there was never a golden moment where these forms existed in the civil service – he cites the 1968 Fulton Report talking about high staff turnover, www.csap.cam.ac.uk/news/article-institutional-memory-decline/
28 Ibid.
29 Based on the personal experiences of Gareth Conyard, who joined in 2003.
30 www.tes.com/magazine/archive/everything-you-need-know-about-education-action-zones
31 Kevin Courtney and Mary Bousted were joint General Secretaries of the NEU from 2017 to 2023, with Kevin serving as Deputy General Secretary of the NUT (one predecessor of the NEU) from 2010, and Mary serving as General Secretary of the ATL (the other predecessor of the NEU) from 2003. Patrick Roach has been General Secretary of the NASUWT since 2020, having served as Deputy for a decade prior. Geoff Barton has been General Secretary of ASCL since 2017 and will serve until 2024. Paul Whiteman has been General Secretary of NAHT since 2017.
32 House of Lords, Education for 11–16 Year Olds Committee, Uncorrected oral evidence: Education for 11–16 year olds, Thursday 13 July 2023. https://committees.parliament.uk/oralevidence/13538/html/
33 https://webarchive.nationalarchives.gov.uk/ukgwa/20111122022029mp_/http://media.education.gov.uk/assets/files/pdf/e/expert%20panel%20pen%20portraits.pdf
34 https://webarchive.nationalarchives.gov.uk/ukgwa/20111123225833/www.education.gov.uk/schools/teachingandlearning/curriculum/a0073091/expert-panel-terms-of-reference
35 Ibid.
36 https://assets.publishing.service.gov.uk/media/5a7b4029ed915d3ed9063285/CM-7980.pdf
37 https://ioelondonblog.wordpress.com/2012/06/12/proposed-primary-curriculum-what-about-the-pupils/
38 https://epi.org.uk/wp-content/uploads/2022/06/Final_report_stuck_schools.pdf
39 https://assets.publishing.service.gov.uk/government/uploads/system/uploads/attachment_data/file/958634/Understanding_Teacher_Retention_Report_by_RAND-February_2021.pdf
40 www.theguardian.com/uk/1999/feb/10/rebeccasmithers
41 www.tes.com/magazine/archive/ofsted-chiefs-all-time-low-remark-riles-2

3 Navigating wider complexity

Education is an extraordinarily complex topic. The interaction of different factors within the education system can be bewildering for individuals and families to navigate as children enter early years provision, move into primary and then secondary school, and on to further and higher education. To some extent, policy-makers have it easier as they tend to look at generalities and large data sets when making decisions, but there is always a point in any policy decision where it comes back to the impact on children and families, where less common and outlier experiences have to be considered. Any policy-maker who loses sight of the impact of any decision on the child in the classroom is going to become unstuck very quickly.

We have already seen how the personal experiences and biases of policy-makers are brought to bear as they navigate the complex waters in which they find themselves, and also how the organisational structures and histories surrounding them help to shape thinking. But education does not sit within a bubble in government nor in society at large, and so as well as trying to grapple with the specific details of education policy, those making judgements and decisions need to do so as they interact with other agendas and factors.

The very name of the Department for Education offers an illustration as to how governments have tried to respond to different priorities over time. From 1839–1964, name changes reflected the gradual elevation of education as a political issue and the fashions of naming conventions of the time, as the Committee of the Privy Council on Education (1839–1856) became the Committee of Council on Education (1856–1900), then the Board of Education (1900–44) and the Ministry of Education (1944–64). Given the wider context of the Harold Wilson Government in 1964, it is no surprise that the Ministry of Education was renamed the Department for Education and Science (DES) in 1964, reflecting the Wilson Government's commitment to technology. After a brief period as simply the Department for Education (DFE) from 1992–95, the Department for Education and Employment (DfEE) was created to attempt to focus more on the link between education and job creation. In 2001, this evolved into the Department for Education and Skills (DfES) to create a distinction between the education aspects of job readiness and the practical operation of Job Centres and so forth, which sat under the auspices of the new Department for Work and Pensions (DWP).

DOI: 10.4324/9781032651057-4

The year 2007 saw perhaps the biggest conceptual shift as – for the first time – the department responsible for education dropped the word from its name, becoming the Department for Children, Schools, and Families (DCSF). In part this was an attempt to refocus the work of the department on the 'end-user' rather than the process, and in part it reflected a policy shift to think about children more holistically as children's social care elements moved into the DCSF and HE and FE policy moved to the new Department of Innovation, Universities, and Skills (DIUS). The 'Every Child Matters' agenda,[1] begun in 2003, reached its culmination under this new structure. Although praised by some, there was a strong reaction against both the agenda and the name change, and when Michael Gove became the Secretary of State for Education in 2010, the department reverted to its current name, the Department for Education (DfE), motivated by Gove's belief that the work of the Department should be focused on the 'core purpose of supporting teaching and learning',[2] and FE and HE policy returned to the fold.

The name of the department might feel like a cosmetic change but it is linked to how we understand the purpose of education – what you think it is for will drive you towards what you prioritise – and it demonstrates how a change in government can bring about a different focus for education policy. This can have a profound impact on decisions made and the tone of engagement with the system, but it has less impact than one might think because, regardless of how a Secretary of State or a government chooses to view the purpose of education, the wider complexities in the system continue to exist. Focusing education policy on teaching and learning is a perfectly reasonable thing for an education minister to attempt to do on the surface of things and indeed many teachers and school leaders would welcome the opportunity to get back to the teaching they were trained to do. But such an approach relies on other necessary support services for children being provided elsewhere.

In May 2023, the education wellbeing charity Education Support published a report that examined the evidence of the modern teacher experience.[3] The evidence showed:

- 74% of teachers often helped pupils with personal matters beyond their academic work
- 33% helped pupils resolve a family conflict
- 26% had prepared food for hungry pupils
- 13% had cleaned pupils' clothes when dirty
- 69% talked to pupils about their mental health
- 41% bought supplies for pupils (pens, paper, bags, etc.)
- 10% bought pupils part of their school uniform

This backdrop helps to explain why comments by Amanda Spielman (then Chief Inspector and leader of Ofsted) created such a strong backlash in the system as she reflected on the impact of the Covid-19 pandemic:

In a lot of schools it felt as though their attention went very rapidly to the most disadvantaged children, into making food parcels, going out visiting …

which may have meant that they did not have the capacity left to make sure there was some kind of education offer for all children.[4]

During the pandemic, teachers were the ones who saw the needs of children and families first hand, who could also see those parents who had nowhere to turn, and who knew that before their children could focus on learning, they needed to be fed, they needed clean clothes, and then they needed paper, pencils, and books. The reality reflected in the research led by Education Support shows clearly that the focus on supporting teaching and learning demanded by Michael Gove back in 2010 is not being felt in schools up and down the country.

From a policy perspective, it is possible to devise an approach to education that tries overtly to integrate and coordinate wider social care issues within schools, as was attempted through 'Every Child Matters' and reflected in the DCSF name, or to have a focus much more tightly defined on teaching and learning, as reflected in the DfE name, with schools relying on others to step in and support wider childhood issues. What will inevitably lead to failure is either an overly complicated system that tries to do too much and loses focus on the educational aspects of schooling, or one that overly simplifies the role of schools while failing to properly fund the wider systems of support. If the rallying cry is to 'let teachers teach' then the system needs to support that.

As we note, the system is complex, subject to change, and full of ambiguities and policy tensions. Effective policy-making and delivery therefore relies on how well decision-makers can navigate this environment, and we suggest there are three ways in which the current modes of operating are making it harder than it needs to be: 'siloing' within the DfE; ineffective cross-government working and unintended consequences; and the failure to build the resilience for 'black swans'.[5]

Siloing within the Department for Education

Regardless of the formal scope of the DfE, like any large organisation its effectiveness will be driven in part by how well it is able to make internal links between policy agendas and ideas. Bureaucracy is often used as a derogatory term but it is essential to ensure the smooth running of things and interchange of information. Bureaucracy can be efficient and positive, or sclerotic and unhelpful: a Rolls Royce or a Reliant Robin.

The DfE is always fighting an uphill battle to avoid dysfunction because of the way the responsibilities of officials and ministers play out in practice. Only the Secretary of State and the Permanent Secretary have oversight of all of the activity of the department, and it is simply impossible for those people – no matter how brilliant they are – to stay across all of the detail and interconnections between different policy areas. The Secretary of State also has wider political responsibilities and invariably has to choose a small number of education policies to focus on, with junior ministers taking on the rest. Put another way, although in theory the Secretary of State is responsible for everything, in practice decision-making is significantly delegated to junior ministers who are not incentivised necessarily to work together to any great degree. The politics of any government are seldom simple, and we should not underestimate the personal animosities that can colour relationships between junior ministers, many of whom may in fact feel they are in competition with their peers to secure promotions. We have already talked about the lack of continuity between different ministerial teams, which adds an additional layer of difficulty in coordinating ideas and activity.

The splits between ministerial roles are reflected in departmental structures, with the most senior management team made up of the Permanent Secretary and their Directors General. They will, of course, talk about areas of common interest and links between areas are possible, but they also have responsibility for the operation of the department, including issues of finance, digital and IT, HR, facilities management, etc. Each Director General also has a wide range of policy responsibilities, each of which will be led by a Director, who again will divide their responsibilities between Deputy Directors. At this stage we are still only talking about the cadre of senior civil servants who represent around 3% of the total number of civil servants in the DfE (as outlined in Chapter 1), and already we have a number of layers of hierarchy and disbursement of responsibilities that make connecting policy ideas difficult. One example: in 2020–21 the Deputy Director responsible for teacher professional development policies reported to a Director (actually a pair of Directors in a jobshare) with wider responsibility for teachers (including terms and conditions, recruitment and retention, wellbeing and workload, amongst other things). There were around 300 people in this directorate. The Director General sitting next up in the chain had the oversight of schools policy, including funding, curriculum, academies, capital (school buildings), inspection, and countless related tasks. Even in the reasonably senior position of Deputy Director, it is near impossible to make links with all those other Deputy Directors to ensure that policy synergies were exploited and challenges prevented. And still we are in the world of schools – what about trying to make a connection with the policy team leading thinking in early years policy or children's social care?[6]

These connections matter because of the complexities within the system, where a change in one area will inevitably have an impact on another. Sometimes interactions are partially managed – for both good and ill. In 2012, consideration was given to awarding Qualified Teacher Status (QTS) to early years teachers in an attempt to raise the status of teaching in the early years and provide parity for this hitherto overlooked group of experts. Links were made internally with wider teacher policy officials who, separately, had been considering an option of removing QTS entirely as a status. The timing of decisions meant that thinking on teachers in schools overrode thinking on early years and even though QTS was never removed and continues to be the cornerstone of teacher training today, the opportunity to expand it into early years was missed. This was a policy connection, but it was asymmetrical and had no longer-term element to the thinking.

This asymmetry is a real challenge for non-schools areas of policy-making. Per-pupil funding tends to be protected by all governments,[7] even as the overall DfE budget has not increased, meaning that savings need to be found from other policy areas. This is a short-term approach that has led directly to the wider challenges now facing schools. As budgets for children's social care services, for Childhood and Adolescent Mental Health Services (CAMHS), and for SEND have shrunk over the past decade and more, so too have issues in those areas emerged, alongside a wider crisis of child poverty. These issues are now being felt in schools, with all the challenges that ensue in terms of workload, recruitment and retention, and school funding.

Teacher workload offers another example of how a lack of join-up within the DfE leads to challenges. It is a commonly cited reason for discontent and inefficiency in the profession, which has led successive governments to pay attention to it. Concerns around teacher workload led the Labour Government to create the National Workforce Agreement in 2003,[8] with a focus on defining the role of the teacher more clearly and specifying what tasks should be undertaken by support staff. Concerns around workload led then Secretary of State Nicky Morgan to launch the Workload Challenge in 2014[9] (which received an astonishing 44,000 responses) and to publish guidance in 2016 on marking, data management, and planning produced in conjunction with Ofsted and the unions.[10] This guidance has been updated several times since that point, and only recently Gillian Keegan has announced the creation of a Workload Reduction Taskforce to tackle workload issues in schools.[11] At least part of the reason why we have been trapped in a repeating pattern of failure is the inability of the department – over a long period of time – to acknowledge that it is itself the biggest driver of workload for schools and teachers and be willing to make compromises to alleviate pressures. The introduction of curriculum reform has driven more workload. The introduction of the Early Career Framework has driven more workload. The accountability regime – both as it operates and every time it is changed – drives more workload. Changes to funding drives more workload. Each of these might be good policies in their own right, but at no point has the department shown real appetite to acknowledge the cumulative impact of frequent and extensive changes to workload, nor to accept that it is one of the reasons why recruitment and retention is such an issue. And, incidentally, a lack of teachers in a school is another significant driver of higher workloads as heads spend more time on recruitment, and other teachers pick up the slack in under-resourced schools.

This is, of course, known by the DfE – by both officials and ministers – but there are few incentives to produce coordinated policy-making over the longer term. The current fad for so-called 'retail politics' creates an environment where politicians are motivated more by political whims than detailed long-termism.

Political whims come in two broad forms: responsive and cosmetic. An example of a responsive whim is the recent debate about increased rates of absence post-pandemic, which appear to show that the number of children – from all backgrounds – missing days of school is increasing.[12] This is not driven by government wish, as in it is not an issue they would seek to promote, but it is something they must respond to. This means policy-making energy shifts to finding solutions to a problem that gets lots of press attention, but not in a way designed to tackle the problem in depth, but rather to make it look like an issue is being tackled. An example of a cosmetic pressure is the recent announcements around Maths to 18, an issue that is of personal interest to Prime Minister Rishi Sunak and which therefore gains traction. It is not that maths has not been seen as an important issue before, but the level of attention and the push for quick announcements means rushed policy-making in the short term, against the knowledge of all involved that a change in Prime Minister is likely to lead to a significant reduction in the salience of the issue. Neither of these types of political whim are based on long-term planning and vision for education, and diminish the capacity for such thinking.

They also highlight a concerning shift in the way the DfE understands its role as the steward of the system. In Chapter 1, we discussed how the principle of 'speaking truth unto power' has become subverted to the idea of 'serving the government of the day' and what this means for individual motivations. But it also has an impact on the organisational structures of the DfE. Against a backdrop of pressure to reduce civil service numbers, whimsical policies nonetheless need to be serviced by officials, which means that other areas of the department lose staff. Ironically, both sides of this equation were demonstrated around the Conservative Party conference in October 2023: as Prime Minister Rishi Sunak announced the creation of a new 'Advanced British Standard' to replace A levels and T levels in due course (which has involved a brand-new focus of work for officials in the DfE),[13] his Chancellor announced a cap on the number of civil servants.[14] In a similar spirit, the recent RAAC crisis meant that civil servants were moved from other policy areas into schools capital to respond to the surge in work. We wonder how many officials were moved from schools capital into previous priority areas (Brexit work, Covid-19, curriculum reform, etc.) and at what cost? Or how the funding team has reduced in size, and whether that will change given public errors made by the DfE in school funding allocations?[15] The civil service says 'Yes, Minister' without the condescending tone implied by Anthony Jay and Jonathan Lynn, and accepts that this means under-resourcing and inconsistency in terms of policy-making and delivery without being honest about that trade-off.

It was always very worrying to sit in meetings at the DfE and realise that civil servants had no overview of the policies that might be impacting on schools. For good reasons, even policies that are developed do not become part of daily practice immediately. Even something as straightforward as bringing in a times tables check in 2017 required development of the check itself, trialling of the questions, consideration of the timing, development of the technology, and making sure that schools had the equipment to run the test. Guidance needed to be written to make sure that all teachers were running the test in the same way before it became mandatory from 2022. But this time lag often means that policy-makers have moved on to thinking about the next policy. There may be other teams with responsibility for evaluation, but too often the communication between teams is poor. This can mean that a group of teachers who have just started to implement a new policy are also being consulted on something different. It can mean that a minister announces a new policy just as those same teachers are taking part in training for a change in a different policy.

We cannot count the number of 'stop' exercises we engaged with to see what we could stop doing to make capacity for new priorities, but we can remember how many things actually stopped: zero. A good example might be the National Teaching Service,[16] which was launched by Nicky Morgan as Secretary of State in 2016, with the aim of incentivising teachers to move into areas of recruitment need. The policy was a failure by any measure and was quickly withdrawn,[17] but still had to be supported as those few teachers who had signed up had been promised funding and support into the future meaning, even into 2019, the civil service was still responsible for the management of the programme. Unsurprisingly, given the lack of any interest in the policy from the top of the office, any argument that we nonetheless needed to ensure we have somebody to manage the winding down of the programme was not welcome.

Ineffective cross-government working and unintended consequences

The only place to start when thinking about cross-government working is HMT – His Majesty's Treasury – although we should be wary of considering HMT as a single entity. It is made up of ministers, political advisors, and civil servants, and is subject to the influences of and engagement with one of the widest sets of stakeholders of any ministry, ranging from economic experts through to all of the sector experts working with individual departments. Nonetheless, there is a strong and coherent institutional view that pervades all at HMT, which can make it act with a unity uncommon in other government departments. Sam Freedman, a former adviser to Michael Gove, talks of this phenomenon as 'Treasury Brain' and describes it as 'endemic to the way we manage public spending. And it needs to change because it's slowly choking us'.[18]

In defence of HMT, it does not operate this way out of spite, but rather because of how it has evolved to understand its purpose. First, at its core, HMT is responsible for managing the public finances, taking care of the money raised by the Crown and ensuring that it is spent wisely. This is a function many centuries in the making, inherited from the early emergence of a centralised state. It is worth remembering that there is seldom (never?) enough money to do all the things that the government wants, and so the body that holds the money automatically has a key role in determining priorities. Second, as the state has become more sophisticated, the role of HMT has shifted from responsive holder of the purse strings to active manager of the economy. To varying degrees and responding to different political philosophies, HMT seeks to influence the wider British economy to the benefit of the taxpayer (i.e. to make the country richer). Both of these roles – holder of public funds and manager of the economy – take HMT into policy-making across government. In education, for example, it means HMT judging whether a particular policy idea represents good value for money when presented by the DfE (e.g. what is the value in investing in better training and development for early years practitioners?) and also pushing for its own policy ideas to support the wider economy (e.g. pushing for early years interventions that increase parental engagement in the labour market).

HMT could be the ultimate long-term player in policy-making, with an agenda that transcends short-term political whims and with an influence far greater than any other player in the system (with the possible exception of Number 10). That it is not is a reflection of a third truism of HMT operation: avoid spending money. HMT is not a spending department and it does not like giving money to spending departments. The austerity agenda imposed by the Coalition Government in 2010 may have been a legitimate political and economic response to the issues flowing from the 2008 financial crisis, but it fed into HMT's worst impulses for control and restraint. Investments by spending departments must meet a high bar for evidence of impact in order to unlock HMT approval, which some might argue promotes effective policy-making (after all, we should not be wasting money on ill-thought-through ideas), but has the effect of stifling innovation and prioritising short-term investments that show quicker returns. And rather than push departments to develop policy better, it often leads to over-promising (saying what needs to be said to get the money) and under-delivery (either because the promised outcomes were never possible or because roll-out is rushed in a race to get the evidence of a successful investment). This of course feeds a cycle of distrust in which HMT stops believing the ideas pushed by departments as they seem to fail more than they succeed, which means tighter HMT control, which means departments respond with even more over-promising and under-delivery.

The key mechanism for HMT control is the annual financial management cycle. Even in times of political stability, with a four to five-year spending review in place (which notionally sets budgets for a parliamentary cycle), there is an annual process of accounting in which HMT scrutinises departmental spending and claws back underspends, which means departments actually operate in annual cycles rather than anything longer term. And it has been some time since we have had anything like a politically stable policy planning cycle, so the lack of longer-term thinking and planning becomes an ever more acute issue.

Number 10 also plays a key role in education policy-making, and the relationships between the ministerial team and key officials and special advisors within the DfE and Number 10 is an important one, but hard to pin down in detail because of the evolving structures and ways of working within Number 10 and across government. Notionally, Number 10 works hand-in-glove with the Cabinet Office to oversee the structures of Cabinet Committees through which cross-government decisions should take place, all supported (from the perspective of education) by the Economic and Domestic Secretariat (EDS) – the group of civil servants who work with key political appointees at the centre of government to manage Cabinet business (including the various sub-committees). EDS also oversees the 'write round' process, by which departments send information about policy decisions in writing to other departments to get permission to proceed. This is the last chance to spot any potential consequences within a policy area, and many officials have ended up rushing around with 48 hours' notice to think about any impacts that might need to be managed.

There have been times when the role of EDS has been crucial and the cabinet system has been a place for genuine discussion, but there are also times when it is largely irrelevant to decision-making and the personal relationships between people in different bits of government become more crucial. Increasingly WhatsApp has become a more common tool than Cabinet Committees for deciding issues. Number 10 does, of course, reflect the personality of the incumbent and you cannot get away from the fact that the competence of the Prime Minister does have an impact on how Number 10 engages with departments and policies. There is little doubt that the Maths to 18 proposals currently being debated by the DfE come straight from Rishi Sunak, who has a personal belief in such a policy. The public inquiry into Covid-19 will show in detail how Boris Johnson's personal views shaped decisions around school closures (or not) during the pandemic.

For officials in the DfE, Number 10 involvement is a double-edged sword. Number 10 can unlock interest and investment, and is the only part of the government that can realistically force HMT into spending when it does not want to. It can also be short term and whimsical, forcing education officials and ministers to chase after different ideas that have no relation to longer-term thinking. Navigating the internal politics can be infuriating and time-consuming, and seldom leads to a better policy idea emerging.

As well as the operational elements of cross-government working, there are of course also policy areas that impact on more than one department. Decisions on the movement of refugees, or changes to the rules on planning permission for housing developments, could bring a sudden increase of families with children into an area, with an inevitable impact on the education provision available. Decisions on business rate increases, or the minimum wage, could impact on the cost of buildings and staff for nurseries. When the government first decided that those who were living in the same house as someone convicted of a sexual offence could be 'disqualified by association', teachers were suddenly faced with the possibility that they could be unable to work because of their partner's or their housemate's conviction, and schools were left with potential gaps in their staffing. This ruling was quickly reversed.

Sometimes policies developed in other departments explicitly require school involvement. Anti-terrorism legislation required teachers to report concerns about children's behaviour under the Prevent duty. Concerns about obesity and lack of physical exercise has led to changes in school meals, as well as opportunities to get involved in sport and to learn about nutrition in the curriculum and outside the school day. These may be worthy initiatives, but they are developed outside the school system, often with little input from those in schools or even education policy-makers, at least in the early stages. If education policy-makers are often unable to understand the impact of policies on teachers in classrooms, those who are developing policies with 'incidental' impacts on the education system are even less likely to realise. While problems of timing (is this being introduced during busy periods or during school holidays?) or lack of guidance are usually picked up before the changes hit schools, it can lead to a lot of scrabbling around by civil servants to reduce the impact. And because the policies are likely to be in the public eye, headteachers in particular will be aware from an early stage that they are going to impact them, but without knowing when or how. This can make the system feel overwhelming for those inside it, leading to cynicism about whether anyone in government really cares about schools.

Some of these issues have been, at least in part, thought through as education policy. Nadhim Zahawi, in his brief spell as Education Secretary in 2021, introduced a range of measures putting climate change at the heart of education,[19] including a new model science curriculum, a National Education Nature Park, and a promise to make school heating 'cleaner and greener'. Much of this may even be welcomed by schools as an important issue to focus on. But it is a policy designed to be shoehorned into an already stretched curriculum by an already exhausted workforce in schools with crumbling concrete, rather than a considered part of a curriculum review, a well-planned professional development strategy, or a thorough review of school buildings. It is also a policy that was introduced at a particular moment in time – in this case to coincide with the government's hosting of the UN Climate Change Summit being hosted by the UK in Glasgow in 2021. With the policy spotlight on climate change, Zahawi was able to get some specific action underway. As the spotlight has moved on, so has the willingness to engage in climate change policies.

Black Swans

Replaying the famous language of former US Defence Secretary Donald Rumsfeld,[20] the lack of coordination within the DfE and across government might be what we can call 'known knowns'. We understand the breadth of responsibility across the department and across government and it is possible – albeit difficult – to find better ways of managing the interactions between different policy areas to ensure greater synergy.

To some extent they also include 'known unknowns' – areas where there may be an understanding of links but no real sense of how consequences may play out: we do not know how a decision to invest in new industry in an area will play out in terms of education, but it might lead to a need for more housing and more schools; it might attract workers from overseas, meaning more EAL provision required; or it might fail to ignite employment, meaning local people move away and school places decline.

Rumsfeld also talked about 'unknown unknowns' – the things that you just cannot predict but that will nonetheless have an impact on what you want to try to achieve. Harold Macmillan summed this up in the famous (and possibly apocryphal) phrase, 'Events, dear boy, events', when describing what might knock a government off course.

Unexpected events are the focus of *The Black Swan* by Nassim Nicholas Taleb in which he describes how the seemingly unpredictable can have such a significant impact on plans and aspirations. Except, of course, there are very few things that are entirely unpredictable – just things that are unlikely or hard to be certain of, and that are difficult to see in the moment. Taleb lays down three conditions for an event to be considered as a Black Swan: first, it must be an outlier, unlike the regular expectations we operate under; second, it must have a significant impact;

and third, we attempt to explain it *post hoc* in a way that makes it intelligible and seemingly predictable.[21]

Against this backdrop, the choice is how far to invest in anticipation and resilience, in things that might never come to pass but that if they did would have a profound impact. Perhaps the best example – and an extremely painful and current one – is the response to the Covid-19 pandemic.

The wider government preparedness for the Covid-19 pandemic is a topic of considerable discussion and controversy, and we will not get into those issues in detail here,[22] but we should consider how far the DfE and the wider education system should have invested in planning ahead of the pandemic. Some of this rests on the extent to which the pandemic could have been predicted, both in terms of happening at all and in terms of its specific impacts, and in both cases we have a mixed answer.

Pandemics have happened before in history, notably the spread of influenza after the end of the First World War, so we should certainly be able to accept the possibility of a pandemic with significant implications for educational provision. But we could reasonably be forgiven for not spending much time thinking about something that had not happened for nigh on a century. What might seem insupportable in hindsight could have felt more reasonable before the Covid-19 pandemic. Except we have more recent examples of pandemic planning, including work undertaken across government, including the predecessor departments to the DfE, to plan for a possible spread of avian flu in the first decade of this century. Does the fact that there has not (yet) been a significant outbreak of avian flu suggest that the planning was worthless?

Let us consider a more extreme example. Suspend your disbelief for a moment and assume that an extraterrestrial race has arrived above Earth, seeking refuge on our planet. They are friendly, welcoming, and keen to integrate. In quick time, England becomes home to tens of thousands of extraterrestrials living in our communities, working in our offices, and attending our schools. Adjustments are made to accommodate differences in physiology, curriculum content, and teaching approaches. We adapt, we learn, we improve, and we move forward. If it happened there would be plenty of those saying it should have been foreseen, that our knowledge of the universe suggests we are not alone, that we know enough about the creation of life to assume similarities amongst all sentient beings in the universe. This example fits the bill for being a Black Swan – it is highly improbable, it would have an extreme impact, and it would be explained away *post hoc*.

Nobody is suggesting the DfE should have a team of officials preparing for the integration of aliens into the education system, nor that the NEU should have a plan in place to recruit alien teachers and protect existing members (maybe a new breakaway union for aliens would form?). The likelihood of the thing occurring is sufficiently minor that it is not worth the effort preparing. But the likelihood of a pandemic occurring was and has always been higher, so the decision to plan in advance comes down to one around risk and prioritisation.

Given what we have already described about the way the DfE – and indeed wider government – operates, there is little incentive to provide resources to consider 'what ifs'. Short-term thinking, reduced funding, and political whimsy reduces the capacity for any organisation to undertake serious thought about something that might not come to pass. The effects of austerity since 2010 (whatever the merits of the policy) reduced both the capacity to plan for unlikely events and the resilience of the system to respond when something unexpected happens. When the Covid-19 pandemic hit, the education system had to be entirely in responsive mode, learning what to do as new information came to light, with examples of significant errors and heroic actions. So, while it is certainly true that there should be a conversation about how we can be better prepared for a future pandemic and the lessons we should learn from the last few years, it should also be true that the DfE – and government across the piece – should pay more attention to the less predictable, the outliers, the Black Swans that might have a fundamental impact upon the provision of education.

Chapter summary

- Education policy-making is complex. There is a significant challenge within education to join up work so that education policies complement one another and do not lead to unintended outcomes.
- Education policy-making does not sit in a vacuum. It is subject to the influence of other policy areas, which can create significant and unintended issues within education if not properly managed.
- In particular, the DfE is subject to decisions made by His Majesty's Treasury (HMT), which tends to drive short-term and unproductive thinking, and Number 10, which operates more on whim than vision.
- Black Swans – unpredictable events – have the capacity to make a major difference to education policy but there is little effort to plan or prepare for the unknown.

Notes

1 https://assets.publishing.service.gov.uk/media/5a7c95a4e5274a0bb7cb806d/5860.pdf
2 http://news.bbc.co.uk/1/hi/uk_politics/8679749.stm
3 www.educationsupport.org.uk/resources/for-organisations/research/teaching-the-new-reality/
4 www.theguardian.com/education/2021/sep/14/ofsted-head-schools-focus-food-parcels-may-have-hit-learning
5 The phrase 'Black Swan' was coined in 2001 by Nassim Nicholas Taleb to describe the impact of unpredictable and improbable events. See Nassim Nicholas Taleb, *The Black Swan* (Penguin, 2010).
6 Based on the personal experiences of Gareth Conyard.
7 www.nao.org.uk/wp-content/uploads/2021/07/School-funding-in-England.pdf
8 https://dera.ioe.ac.uk/id/eprint/540/1/081210thenationalagreementen.pdf
9 https://assets.publishing.service.gov.uk/media/5a7f0c7ded915d74e6228124/Government_Response_to_the_Workload_Challenge.pdf
10 www.gov.uk/government/publications/teacher-workload-poster-and-pamphlet
11 www.gov.uk/government/groups/workload-reduction-taskforce
12 www.publicfirst.co.uk/public-first-research-finds-parental-support-for-fulltime-schooling-has-collapsed.html

13 www.conservatives.com/news/2023/cpc23-address-from-rishi-sunak
14 www.gov.uk/government/news/end-to-civil-service-expansion-and-review-of-equality-a
    nd-diversity-spending-announced-in-productivity-drive
15 https://schoolsweek.co.uk/dfe-made-370m-error-in-school-funding-calculations/
16 www.gov.uk/guidance/national-teaching-service-for-teachers-and-middle-leaders
17 https://schoolsweek.co.uk/national-teaching-service-cancelled-after-just-24-accept-places/
18 https://samf.substack.com/p/defeating-treasury-brain
19 www.gov.uk/government/news/education-secretary-puts-climate-change-at-the-heart-of
    -education-2
20 Donald Rumsfeld, then US Secretary of Defence, at a NATO press conference, 6 June
    2002, www.nato.int/docu/speech/2002/s020606g.htm
21 Nassim Nicholas Taleb, *The Black Swan* (Penguin, 2010).
22 https://covid19.public-inquiry.uk/

4   What can we learn from the recent past?

It is important to understand the personal traits, organisational dynamics, and long-term and wider trends that shape policy-making, but when it comes to thinking about how to make things better we must start from a pragmatic understanding of how things are now. Attractive as it might be to sit down with a blank piece of paper and draft a more ideal solution, change must be rooted in what is real if it is to be effective. In particular, at this moment in time on the cusp of an election in which Labour are expected to win, there will be those hoping for a quick return to the ways of working in place before the 2010 general election. Although we think it is both impossible and a mistake to simply revert to the pre-2010 election circumstances, there are lessons from the recent history of education policy-making that help us to understand what is practicable now, from the days of New Labour, through the coalition, and into the current government.

We are interested here in *how* policy has been made over the last two decades – focusing on conscious efforts to create better processes rather than the detail of policy-making and delivery. This could be considered through the lens of Kahneman's system 1 and system 2 thinking[1] – the deliberate and laudable efforts (system 2 thinking) to try to create structures and processes that automatically (system 1 thinking) lead to better outcomes.

There are three themes that we explore in this chapter: first, the use of and then dismantling of the quasi-autonomous non-governmental organisation (Quango) approach; second, social partnership; and third, policy-making frameworks, especially from government.

It takes two to quango

The use of publicly funded but somewhat independent bodies to deliver government policy is not new but it has become less fashionable. According to a 2010 research paper from the House of Commons Library:

> Since it was coined in the 1970s, 'quango' has become a highly emotive term. For many it is a byword for wasteful bureaucracy, patronage and lack of democratic accountability. It is no surprise that politicians from all sides have regularly called for reductions in their number, expenditure and influence.[2]

DOI: 10.4324/9781032651057-5

Nick Gibb has been a vocal critic of the use of quangos, as shown by this exchange with one of his predecessors, Jim Knight:

> Lord Knight of Weymouth: Within the context of a knowledge-rich curriculum, is it right that Ministers are the people who decide what the right knowledge is to deliver cultural literacy to children in this country? Should that be something that professional experts agree on?
>
> Nick Gibb: Yes, because we live in a parliamentary democracy. The alternative is that you hand it over to experts who are not accountable to the public in any way to make those decisions. We saw that with the QCDA in your time, when it made decisions that I did not feel even Ministers were on top of. It certainly was not accountable to this place. It was not accountable to committees such as this or the Education Committee in the Commons.[3]

Such a view will come as no surprise to those who have worked with Nick Gibb, and it is fair to say that the previous Labour Government was more comfortable creating and using arm's-length bodies than the current Conservative Government. This does not mean that Labour under Blair and Brown did not believe in political oversight but rather that it did not view the use of quangos as diminishing that ultimate responsibility.

Given the concerns about quangos and the bad press they have received, why have they been popular at all? Despite their often-negative portrayal now, they were seen as a key way to drive efficiency and improve the operation of government, including by the Thatcher administration through its embracing of the so-called 'Next Steps' process.[4] One of the key benefits is the ability to create a formalised structure for engaging with experts and the evidence to form decisions that are more broadly accepted and seen as less political. This is always a challenge as these bodies influence public policy, often making decisions on the allocation of public funding. It is worth being clear that they still exist, albeit with different nomenclature and oversight arrangements, in the form of non-departmental public bodies (NDPBs) or arm's-length bodies (ALBs), each with a specific relationship with a parent government department. Even the fiercest critics of them do not want them to cease to exist, but are interested in how to exert control and influence.

We can think about how this has changed by considering policies around assessment, qualifications, and curriculum. From 1988 (when the National Curriculum Council (NCC) was formed) through to 2010, when the decision was made to dissolve the Qualifications and Curriculum Development Agency (QCDA),[5] curriculum policy was led with a degree of independence from ministers. The direction shifted in 2010 when assessment functions moved to the Standards and Testing Agency (STA), which is an Executive Agency of the DfE (which means it is fully integrated into the department, staffed by civil servants, and its Chief Executive reports to the Director General for Schools). The qualification functions moved to Ofqual (a non-ministerial department that regulates the provision of qualifications and reports directly to Parliament, the same as Ofsted). And the curriculum functions moved directly within the DfE.

The degree of autonomy present before 2010 fed a more consultative and open process of curriculum reform, but undoubtedly did so at the expense of direct ministerial control. For some this made it more democratic – it engaged a wider range of people in genuine attempts to reach consensus. For others it made it less democratic as elected politicians had less direct control. The use of NPDBs also raises questions about the principle of ministerial accountability – the notion that a minister will take responsibility, including resigning, for mistakes in their remit even if they did not have direct control.

For example, the School Curriculum and Assessment Authority (SCAA) was independent of government, but there were regular meetings with civil servants and ministers to share information and shape ideas. As part of its assessment responsibility, SCAA officials supported statutory assessment in primary schools, administering the contracts for the organisations that developed the tests and evaluated them, keeping on top of issues of 'cheating', and then bringing to publication the 'Reports to Schools'. This report built on the evaluations and gave teachers insights into the ways in which children answered particular questions, and highlighted where topics appeared to be less well taught or where particular groups of children struggled. When contracts were awarded, those decisions were reported to ministers, and regular meetings with civil servants meant that they were aware of the test developers' progress towards getting the tests written, delivered, marked, and reported, as well as any potential problems. This continued when SCAA became QCA (the Qualifications and Curriculum Authority) in 1998. When one of those contractors involved in test marking failed in that same year, although ostensibly QCA's responsibility, questions were asked in Parliament and there were calls for the then Secretary of State to resign.[6]

It is worth noting that similar issues have arisen since the STA came into being directly within the DfE. Two data breaches during the 2016 SATs cycle meant that the DfE cancelled one test (the Key Stage 1 Spelling, Punctuation, and Grammar) and had to provide significant reassurance for another. Nick Gibb took responsibility in Parliament and had closer control over the issue due to the nature of his relationship overseeing the STA within the DfE, but nonetheless did not resign over the errors which were the responsibility of the STA, instead announcing a 'root-and-branch' review which reported in November 2016.[7]

One of the benefits of using a body at arm's length is that a group of experts can take time to deliberate over the issues, to develop, implement, and evaluate policy away from the daily vicissitudes of politics. When the QCA developed the first Foundation Stage curriculum for children up to the age of five, it brought together a range of early years experts to develop each area of learning and also to meet together to integrate the areas of learning and ensure a coherent curriculum. Those experts were practitioners and researchers, making sure that the curriculum was founded on evidence but that it would also work in different types of early years classrooms. The work was led by a respected expert in the early years, who was also very good at political negotiation. Working with the experts, she developed a clear plan for the curriculum, led a process of widespread consultation, and engaged with ministers at important points to share emerging thinking and take on board concerns from ministers (especially around messaging). Having expert groups over a long period of time allowed QCA to go from consultation with practitioners through development of the principles and the collection of evidence into detailed conversations about the structure and content of the curriculum. Having practitioners in settings in those groups gave confidence that the curriculum could work in practice. For ministers interested in seeing improvements in the system, relying on the QCA meant accepting a slower pace and a loss of control, putting faith in a trade-off that it would nonetheless lead to better outcomes.

The demise of the QCDA and other NDPBs has not stopped the use of experts to help shape policy but it has changed the locus of power in determining the scope and membership of expert bodies. Rather than established agencies with clear remits and powers, issues that require broader engagement are instead led by expert groups convened for a specific purpose. An example is the Tickell Review of the Early Years Foundation Stage (EYFS) in 2011,[8] in which Dame Claire Tickell was given a brief by and reported directly to the Secretary of State. Subsequent changes to the EYFS, most recently in 2021,[9] were led directly by civil servants, relying on stakeholder engagement to work with the profession.

As we set out in Chapter 2, the use of policy networks tends to lead to an over-reliance on working with those who agree with you, who already share your worldview and are interested in pursuing the same policy goals as you are, which reduces the scope for independent challenge and new ideas. A further problem with the way in which people are selected is that those who are 'well known' are often a self-selecting group. When the NEU set up the Independent Assessment Commission in 2021, it quickly became clear that it was very difficult to identify experts in assessment, qualifications, and exams who were from minority ethnic groups, because most of those who hold important positions are white and often male. There are many reasons why this might be, including the increasingly cited concern that people from global majority backgrounds may be valued for their expertise on diversity, but not for their intellectual or academic expertise. And it becomes a vicious circle when the experts who debate decisions and make policy recommendations come from a narrow selection of the population.

There have been many instances over the years where the groups discussing policies that will impact on classroom practice contain no teachers. Or where all those with backgrounds in schools are from Multi-Academy Trusts or schools judged 'outstanding' by Ofsted. Or, as *Schools Week* pointed out with reference to the teacher workload groups announced in October 2015, where expert teachers are predominantly from the south of England: nineteen from the south against only nine from the north.[10] Increasingly, the same names crop up time and again. We are not questioning the expertise of the people chosen, nor making judgements on the types of schools or roles that they occupy. What is clear though is that it is very difficult to have conversations that identify particular assumptions or biases if all participants have similar backgrounds. It is too easy to develop policies that will not work well in small schools, or for pupils with profound and multiple learning difficulties, or in reception classes, if those on the expert groups have no experience of these things. It is possible to hear evidence from a group of teachers from rural schools or large inner city secondary schools, but without a champion for those views on the expert group, it is just as easy to forget that evidence as conclusions are forming, and have to reverse-engineer policies somehow.

Social partnership

There have been times when government and unions have worked closely together in developing education policy. One of these was the School Workforce Partnership in the early 2000s, bringing the trade unions representing teachers, leaders, and support staff, alongside employers, into the heart of government policy development. Teacher and school leader workload had been acknowledged as a growing issue for the New Labour Government from the beginning of their first term in 1997, leading to the publication of Circulars and the commissioning of PwC to look into the issue. Teacher recruitment was going down, unions were threatening industrial action, and the Labour Government decided it was time to move beyond the confrontations that characterised relationships with unions and attempt to build a more consensual way of working. As Mary Bousted noted, when General Secretary of ATL: 'The Social Partnership came at the only time it could have emerged, both because of what had gone before and the renewed emphasis on education.'[11]

This needed intense discussions, both between ministers, senior civil servants, and union general secretaries, but also within the unions themselves. Following over a year of discussions, government and unions signed *The National Agreement on Raising Standards and Tackling Workload* on 15 January 2003.[12] In the end this did not include all unions, as the National Union of Teachers (NUT) pulled out of the negotiations before the Agreement was signed and the National Association of Headteachers (NAHT) left and then rejoined part way through. However, the partnership lasted until the May 2010 General Election brought in a Conservative/Liberal Democrat Coalition Government.

The Workforce Agreement set the parameters for partnership work. The intense discussion before it was signed meant that partners came to the table clear about the intentions, and that all partners had also gained commitment from their members, for unions and employers, and from across government, to the principles and plans that would be carried out. This included commitment to the government's 'workforce remodelling' agenda and its drive towards 'new professionalism'. For the unions, this commitment was not easy to gain, nor to maintain, and there were regular debates at annual conferences and in Executive Meetings, with members calling for their leadership to exit the partnership, but it embodied enough of a shared vision of the future that union leadership was able to remain committed.

The Agreement also gave rise to the Workforce Agreement Monitoring Group (WAMG – generally pronounced 'Wham-Gee'), bringing the signatories and others as necessary together to monitor the impact of the actions to reduce workload. It established an independent Implementation Review Unit to consider the impact of new policies and initiatives from DfES, QCA, the Teacher Training Agency (TTA), and Ofsted on workload, and to bear down on excessive bureaucracy. The Rewards and Incentives Group (RIG) emerged in 2004 to agree changes to the School Teachers' Pay and Conditions Document (STPCD) related to leadership group and post-Threshold teachers, and involved the partners developing joint evidence to the School Teachers' Review Body (STRB). The Agreement was also supported by a National Remodelling Team. In short, the department created a wider supportive bureaucracy to ensure that ongoing and open conversations took place between government and unions on what became an increasingly wide range of topics, as almost all policy ideas needed to be considered in terms of the impact on workload.

Between all parties, this was a huge commitment, involving weekly meetings, often taking whole days. Meetings were held at the DfE, in the offices of the different unions, and at neutral venues. Beyond that, there would be frequent meetings and conversations between partner unions as well as many meetings within the individual unions in order to make sure that union policies were being adhered to. Monitoring included RAG rating the implementation (using a Red/Amber/Green system to identify where changes were being made or not), with problems taken to the minister, along with the expectation from government that unions would become involved in schools where implementation was causing problems.

Debbie Christophers, in her comprehensive account of social partnership for the NASUWT, sets out three principles that the Partnership operated under.[13] First, that the government had the mandate to govern and would set the direction. This meant that there was still some hierarchy within the partnership, and it was possible for difficult issues to be escalated to a minister for a final decision, although this was rare. Second, nothing was agreed until everyone agreed. This often meant that discussions were enormously detailed and operational. Partners would come with their 'red lines', issues on which they were not willing to compromise, where they believed they would lose the support of members. It also meant that there were many meetings in between the weekly WAMG meetings, so that union officials could hammer out possible ways forward within their own organisations and then with other partners, working out where the alliances were and what were the underlying reasons for disagreement. It made for very slow progress on some issues, but ensured that all partners would support the final outcome. And finally, all discussions were confidential. This allowed the partners to discuss policy at very early stages of thinking, in the knowledge that even the silliest sounding ideas could be put on the table without being on the front page of the news.

According to Ed Balls, former Labour Secretary of State for Children, Schools and Families:

> The fact that we would engage with social partners substantially ahead of any policy decision making was fundamental and the time spent with senior representatives meant we undoubtedly achieved better policy outcomes. The process and the trust we had meant that when we amended things we did so with the confidence that the profession was behind us and when we made mistakes we discussed them face to face, rather than being publicly lambasted in the press.[14]

Because so much of the Agreement was focused on remodelling the workforce, it led to a national change management programme. Although this involved working closely with schools, it was along the lines of road testing the remodelling process with a small number of schools before a national roll-out. Schools were trained in the process and given tools and techniques which could then be adapted to their own contexts and practices. The remodelling team reported to WAMG, which gave an enormous amount of school-level data for them to consider. While this was still, in some ways, a process of being 'done to', it built up the skills and cultures within schools to manage change and the 'permission' to use and adapt resources as needed rather than being told exactly what to do by government. At the time, this was a very different process to the way in which schools would previously have been expected to manage directives from the government.

While the social partnership was an important way of co-creating policy, it had a number of problems. Although confidentiality allowed much more free discussion between senior officials, it also meant being unable to discuss some aspects of policy with members until the policy was finalised, which led to disconnection with members both in discussions and in outcomes. This was linked to the need for unanimity between partners with different perspectives and ideologies, which led to compromises that could leave some members worse off or disagreeing with a policy that their union was now obliged to promote. Confidentiality meant that unions were unable to show their members what might have been imposed upon them without engagement with the partnership. As Stephenson, Carter, and Passy point out:

> ... critics (NUT, 2003; Thompson, 2006) argue that a high price has been paid for this improved relationship with the government. Unions have accepted the principle of those without qualified teacher status teaching whole classes and have also found themselves having to defend proposals resulting in pay cuts for members and increasingly onerous appraisal arrangements. More significant is the extent to which this closer relationship with government may have impaired unions' ability to act independently in defence of their members' interests.[15]

In operational terms, partnership working took a lot of time and made slow progress. There was a lot of poring over data and focusing on details of implementation, which also meant that data needed to be collected in schools. This led to changes in focus in schools around what was measured and collected, and also put the government along with the partners in a relationship of monitoring and intervening from the centre. It was too easy to get caught up in detailed monitoring of school workload rather than the broader work of identifying trends and developing policy to improve the situation.

And it exposed differences in the priorities of the different partners. A large proportion of discussion arose because of those different priorities: headteachers wanting to retain autonomy and control with their schools or teachers wanting the protection of policy against the decisions of school leaders; unions representing support staff wanting enhanced professional roles for their members or those representing teachers not wanting to lose jobs for their supply teacher members. Government remained 'in control', with the mandate to govern, and officials were aware that their role was to implement ministerial objectives. While the partnership involved the government conceding some of their power, and officials were as involved in discussion and compromise as the other partners, it worked because (in the main) all partners were committed to the outcomes. Where disagreements arose which could not be resolved, the option remained for ministers to be the final arbiter. And partners could leave, as the NAHT did, although the asymmetry is clear here too: had the government chosen to leave, the partnership would have ceased to exist.

Of course, some of those problems were also benefits. Different groups of workers will always have different needs and interests, and partnership brought the opportunity to work together to bring these into the open and to try to build solutions rather than being confrontational and allowing solutions to be imposed. It forced the unions in particular to articulate more clearly what they were for and not just what they were against. The partnership enabled greater influence over policy-making, particularly for the smaller unions. It gave everyone a better understanding of the compromises that needed to be made, not just between the competing priorities of unions or unions and government, but also between the different priorities of government, and within the available funding. It built closer relationships between union officials too, both at senior level and at the level of those who were doing the detailed work, helping them to better understand the issues where they could work together to benefit their members and the children and young people they worked with. And it enabled closer working between the government and the unions at the early stages of policy development, when changes are still possible; this involved working together to explore the problems and to identify and consider a range of possible solutions rather than being presented with a defined problem and its favoured solution and being invited to support teachers to implement it. Even the slow progress could be seen as a benefit: governments like to be seen to be taking decisive action, making fast changes, but too often that leads to policies being implemented too quickly and without adequate thought or resources. A slower pace of policy-making allows for better policies and gives teachers time to implement one before the next one hurtles down the line. It might even give policy-makers time to evaluate the impacts and make changes.

Social partnership was abandoned in 2010, and initially nothing replaced it. Engagement with the unions became sporadic on particular issues, and it was not until 2014 that a regular routine was re-established with the introduction of the Programme of Talks. These were regular (generally monthly) meetings between civil servants and union officials with the occasional visit from ministers, Ofsted, and others. Agendas were formed as the talks progressed, with no sense of long-term planning (certainly not beyond 9–12 months) and no intention to meaningfully engage in joint decision-making or policy development. There were opportunities for civil servants to share early thinking about problems and solutions, but these were more likely to involve union officials offering different interpretations of the data, different perspectives on the views of those working in schools, and criticising proposed solutions. And there was no requirement for officials to take any of these ideas on board or to make any compromises or changes. Relationships reverted to the confrontational, and conversations to the rehearsal of pre-planned 'set piece' arguments. Any progress made was likely to be behind-the-scenes work as officials both for unions and government tried to find mutually beneficial solutions and avoid unhelpful confrontations and grandstanding by both ministers and general secretaries.[16]

Critics would argue that this lack of positive and considered engagement has helped to create the deplorable situation around teacher recruitment and retention, workload, mental health, and pay, as government has failed to properly work with and understand the system it governs. On the other side, the amount of government-led change in the education system over the last decade and more has been helped by avoiding the need to get negotiated approval from unions in advance of making decisions.

Civil service changes to policy-making

Since its inception as a modern organisation following the 1854 Northcott-Trevelyan report,[17] the civil service has evolved and reformed to respond to changing demands and fashions. The 1968 Fulton Report sought to create a modern and responsive service,[18] and in the 1980s Thatcher oversaw fundamental changes in the relationships between the civil service and ministers, not least through the processes of privatisation and the creation of separate departmental approaches to recruitment and remuneration.[19] Work continues to the present day, with former Cabinet Office minister Frances Maude commissioned to review civil service governance and accountability in 2022,[20] with emerging thinking reported already.[21]

This work is so important because although policy-making relies on the involvement of the whole system in order to be effective, it must recognise the power dynamics: government holds the purse strings and makes final decisions, and the civil service is the policy arm of government.

The 1999 *Modernising Government* White Paper was the Blair administration's first attempt to change the way policy was made and enacted.[22] This identified some problems which will sound familiar today: policies that are developed without proper collaboration or cooperation across departments or across regional and national government; and an increasing separation between policy-making and delivery, which meant that those who are involved on the frontline were not sufficiently involved in the development of policy. The White Paper led to a range of workstreams and organisational changes that attempted to improve the policy-making process across government, which collectively found their form in the ways of working of the Blair administration, in many ways typified by the career of Sir Michael Barber who played such a pivotal role during the New Labour years, first as Chief Advisor to David Blunkett, then as head of the Prime Minister's Delivery Unit from 2001–2005.

In his excellent book *How to Run a Government,* [23] Sir Michael Barber sets out his own set of practical steps those working in government should take to get things done, a concept he refers to as 'Deliverology' with a key focus on using the mechanisms and influences of government to act. For civil servants, there is a lot to recommend in this approach with practical ideas around the effective use of targets to focus minds and monitor performance, for example, but it is focused on the role of government specifically rather than on the wider set of actors and systems that we know impact on outcomes for those in education. Of the 57 rules he proposes at the end of the book, none are overtly about working collaboratively with the wider sector, and several are framed in the expectation of antagonism. For example, in the section on prioritising, Sir Michael suggests, in rule 7, that governments should 'Consult without conceding on ambition (opposition is inevitable)'.[24] Such an approach bakes in the notion of oppositional policy-making from the very beginning of a process, and places the power to effect change primarily in the hands of government rather than spreading it more effectively across the system. It reflects the assumptions that the Blair administration made (and often found to be true) about finding reluctance and opposition to change. When considering how to organise effectively, Sir Michael proposes rule 12, 'Create a guiding coalition for each priority (to increase clarity and speed.)'[25] and promisingly talks about just such a coalition through the lens of an education policy – improving literacy and numeracy. Yet the coalition described is narrow and defensive – ensuring alignment between ministers, civil servants, and the Delivery Unit at No. 10, with no consideration of the much larger group of organisations and people needed to actually deliver the policy changes – schools, teachers, leaders, unions, parents, etc.

You could imagine a book like Sir Michael's existing for all the different players in the system – unions, think tanks, schools, teachers, etc. – all focused on how to maximise their impact towards their own specific agendas. In each case, the rules proposed would seek to advance the particular sectional interest of each organisation, including how to 'win' in conflict with other education sector organisations. We would argue that it does not mean that ideas for collaboration under the Labour Government – most specifically in the case of education the social partnership – were not genuine, but more that there was always a level of protection in case things went wrong, and a concern that they would.

Civil service approaches to policy-making did not feel change in 2010 even as policies themselves changed. Sir Michael Barber, for example, has continued to advise Conservative governments in different roles, and we are still looking at different options for improving the nature of policy-making and delivery. As well as the work that Frances Maude has been commissioned to do, noted above, many others with experience of the system have written about the inability of the civil service to make better policy., For example, former Permanent Secretary of the

DfE, Jonathan Slater (who was unceremoniously ditched from his position following issues with A level grades in 2020[26]) diagnoses the central problem as 'Whitehall's remoteness from the public and frontline results in policy-making which is fundamentally inadequate to address the challenges we face.'[27]

Attempts to improve policy-making have been frequent and still exist. Civil servants are able to go on policy-making courses and there is a dedicated learning portal – Civil Service Learning – with online courses including on policy-making and delivery. Aspiring and current senior leaders can take part in the Future Leaders Scheme or Senior Leaders Scheme, and there are training programmes targeted at Directors and Directors General.[28] The Infrastructure and Projects Authority (part of the Cabinet Office) oversees its own programme of training for the successful delivery of major projects – the Major Projects Leadership Academy.[29] The civil service identifies those who exist within the 'policy profession' and has cross-government programmes of improvement.[30] When he was Permanent Secretary of the DfE, Jonathan Slater promoted a set of policy tests that all civil servants must consider when framing advice and delivering policy,[31] all designed to improve the process.

So why is it not working? One of the key reasons is that many of the lessons about how to make and deliver better policy smash against the realities of political timetables, cross-government compromises, and – being frank when considering recent governments – the competence of Secretaries of State and Prime Ministers when it comes to effective policy-making. For example, a common theme amongst many training programmes is to develop a realistic timetable for implementation, including thinking about who to involve and when, how to communicate change, and how to build in redundancy for when things go wrong. Against ever-pressing timescales and resource constraints, programmes with enough people, time, and resources are incredibly rare and, as noted in Chapter 1, the lived reality of being a civil servant means advice to ministers saying something cannot be done is a form of career suicide. We suggest it is no coincidence that Jonathan Slater was the first Permanent Secretary to demand a 'Letter of Direction' over policy reform from the then Secretary of State for Education, Damien Hinds,[32] and then found a severe lack of support from ministers a few years later. Improving policy-making is not just about civil service reform – it has to be about reform across the whole of government and the wider system, including how ministers (and special advisers) operate.

Chapter summary

- Any improvements to policy-making have to take account of the recent past – what is the foundation on which change needs to be built?
- One of these is the shift away from using quangos, with a concentration of power in central government seen as either more or less democratic depending on your perspective.

- Another is to learn from the experience of social partnership and to understand how other forms of engagement lead to quicker but less considered results.
- And it is important to understand the largely failed attempts to improve the policy-making skills within the civil service.

Notes

1 Daniel Kahneman, *Thinking Fast and Slow* (Penguin, 2011).
2 www.parliament.uk/globalassets/documents/commons/lib/research/key_issues/Key-Issues-Quangos.pdf
3 House of Lords, Education for 11–16 Year Olds Committee, Thursday 13 July 2020, https://committees.parliament.uk/oralevidence/13538/html/
4 www.civilservant.org.uk/library/1988_improving_management_in_government_the%20_next_steps.pdf
5 The NCC became the School Curriculum and Assessment Authority (SCAA) in 1993 (as it merged with the Schools Examinations and Assessment Council (SEAC, also created in 1988)). This in turn became the Qualification and Curriculum Authority (QCA) in 1997 with the merger of the SCAA and the National Council for Vocational Qualifications (NCVQ), and finally became the Qualifications and Curriculum Development Agency, before it was dissolved in 2011.
6 Based on the first-hand experience of Nansi Ellis,
7 www.gov.uk/government/publications/standards-and-testing-agency-review-final-report-and-sta-response
8 https://assets.publishing.service.gov.uk/media/5a7ac0ec40f0b66a2fc02915/DFE-00177-2011.pdf
9 www.gov.uk/government/publications/changes-to-the-early-years-foundation-stage-eyfs-framework
10 https://schoolsweek.co.uk/south-dominates-workload-groups/
11 Debbi Christophers, *Inside Social Partnership: Transforming the School Workforce (2003–2010)* (NASUWT, date not specified), www.nasuwt.org.uk/static/uploaded/76a6565c-77a8-4358-9e2cb5e46a92f1af.pdf
12 https://dera.ioe.ac.uk/id/eprint/540/1/081210thenationalagreementen.pdf
13 Debbi Christophers, *Inside Social Partnership: Transforming the School Workforce (2003–2010)* (NASUWT, date not specified), p. 16, www.nasuwt.org.uk/static/uploaded/76a6565c-77a8-4358-9e2cb5e46a92f1af.pdf
14 Ibid., p. 5.
15 https://journals.library.ualberta.ca/iejll/index.php/iejll/article/view/670/331 (p. 7)
16 As an aside, this was how your authors met.
17 www.civilservant.org.uk/library/1854_Northcote_Trevelyan_Report.pdf
18 https://civilservant.org.uk/csr-fulton_report-findings.html
19 www.civilservant.org.uk/csr_detail-note1.html
20 www.gov.uk/government/news/lord-maude-to-lead-review-into-civil-service-governance-and-accountability
21 www.instituteforgovernment.org.uk/comment/francis-maudes-review-whitehall
22 www.civilservant.org.uk/library/1999_modernising_government.pdf
23 Michael Barber, *How to Run a Government so That Citizens Benefit and Taxpayers Don't Go Crazy* (Allen Lane, 2015).
24 Ibid., p. 22.
25 Ibid., p. 57.
26 www.civilserviceworld.com/professions/article/dfe-perm-sec-jonathan-slater-sacked-over-a-level-row
27 www.kcl.ac.uk/policy-institute/assets/fixing-whitehalls-broken-policy-machine.pdf

28 www.gov.uk/government/publications/civil-service-talent-management/civil-service-tale nt-management
29 https://assets.publishing.service.gov.uk/media/5dea3512e5274a06d662b1b8/MPLA_ Handbook_for_IPA_Website__2_.pdf
30 https://publicpolicydesign.blog.gov.uk/2022/05/12/new-strategy-for-policy-design/
31 https://quarterly.blog.gov.uk/2013/07/12/the-policy-tests-transforming-policy-in-the- department-for-education/
32 www.civilserviceworld.com/professions/article/dfe-perm-sec-gets-ministerial-direction- to-press-ahead-with-technical-education-reforms

5   What can we learn from international examples?

Seeking international examples of better policy-making is both essential and maddening. The idea that we are not dealing with similar issues as others around the world is clearly nonsensical and to limit ourselves in experience and wisdom is to limit our ambition. Yet, policy-making is inevitably tied very closely to political and social systems, to the context in which you are operating, so it is never straightforward to attempt to take an idea from one place and make it successful in another. It misses historical differences and the nuanced relationships within political and educational systems. A process that might work in a country with a system of coalition government built on compromise and co-production may fare far less well in the UK's 'winner takes all' election system. Similarly, it is possible that in smaller nations, ordinary people, teachers, and researchers have closer ties with policy-makers and politicians than in larger nations like England.

The task, therefore, is to seek to learn but not replicate, to understand fundamental principles and ideas and consider how they might be adapted for our own context. Be wary of anyone who promises a straightforward 'cut-and-paste' approach to any policy challenge and fails to explain how adaptations will respond to the circumstances of the English education system.

The other significant issue is, of course, that the world is vast and any attempt to understand the different approaches in every country is doomed to fail. Being selective is essential and, through that process of selection, biases and opportunism emerge. Why look at a particular country? Are you looking to find an example that validates or challenges your existing views?[1]

This chapter contains international examples that are selected to conform with the broad themes we are exploring in this book. It would create an odd narrative if they did not and jarred with the line of argument elsewhere. We want to own this bias and accept that there are other examples that people can cite that suggest contrary strands of thinking. We are also limited to reading reports rather than being personally engaged, which will also give a particular view. Nonetheless we believe the examples explored here inspire and challenge our thinking on how to develop better ways to make education policy. We have looked for examples that illuminate in three broad themes: How do other jurisdictions bring people into the policy-making process? How do they learn and improve policy? And how do they think about the future?

DOI: 10.4324/9781032651057-6

Bringing people together

The Organisation for Economic Co-operation and Development (OECD) has thought hard about promoting more open government, where citizens are deliberately involved in decision-making. In a 2020 publication it suggests we need new ways to make decisions, find common ground and take action, 'particularly true for issues that are values-based, require trade-offs, and demand long-term solutions'.[2] The report suggests a number of benefits that accrue if a deliberative and representative approach is taken, including better outcomes overall that are considered to be more legitimate, leading to increased public trust in politicians and institutions, and outcomes that are more inclusive.

In the same report the OECD has also drawn together a set of good practice principles to guide deliberative decision-making so that countries can reflect on how to take these ideas on board. They include: governments being clear on the intention of engagement and committing to respond to the recommendations made, so that people know the point and worth of engaging; being transparent, sharing papers and evidence openly; being inclusive, with a particular focus on engaging marginalised or under-represented groups; allowing the proper time for engagement and deliberation; ensuring the privacy of individuals involved; and building in open evaluation approaches.

Estonia's approach to consultative policy-making

While many countries – including England – are committed to consulting its citizens about policies, some have begun to go further. Estonia has long had an online platform where citizens could comment on legislative drafts, although those drafts were often only available a few weeks before they were approved, allowing limited time for public involvement. The Estonian Government has regularly reviewed and improved the platform, including through training for those who use it, and in the past few years has begun to move beyond consultation towards co-creation of policy. According to the Open Government Partnership,[3] civil servants wanted to be able to co-create legislation across the different ministries, and there was a desire to involve citizens earlier in the process of policy development. In 2020, the government committed to developing the system as a collaborative environment where civil servants can work on the same documents together and with experts outside government, and to build online spaces for discussion and working groups. The commitment included developing better processes for alerting the public as soon as policy-making begins so that comments could be made even before the drafts were available to read. This means that citizens can be involved in all stages of policy-making, as observers of a transparent process and as active participants through the ability to comment on proposals and through participating in working groups.

Estonia has not come suddenly to this kind of citizen participation. There has long been an expectation that policy-making must involve all those who are affected by the policies developed in order to achieve 'social agreement'.

Government departments regularly bring together commissions of interested people to discuss problems and solutions and to engage with experts and policy-makers. In developing their Forestry Plan,[4] for example, the Ministry of the Environment convened a people's forest assembly of 50 self-nominated representatives. There are also opportunities for individuals to submit policy proposals directly to Parliament, either nationally where ideas must have the support of at least 1,000 other people, or locally where the proposal must have the support of at least 1% of those eligible to vote in the local area.

The Estonian government seems to have found it helpful to build a process that encourages their citizens to become involved in policy-making. In particular it seems that 'social agreement' is a way of ensuring that ordinary people become committed to the outcomes of policies. In developing their Forestry Plan in this way, Estonia understands that: 'Disagreements and conflicts of interest may arise during the preparation of the development document'. As they point out:

> With the help of the involvement of interest groups, good thoughts, solutions and expert opinions can be collected for the preparation of a high-quality end result and for making justified choices. A well-thought-out and well-implemented involvement creates the assumption that the forestry development plan will be prepared by considering the proposals of all interest groups and will receive the approval of the Riigikogu [Parliament].[5]

From England's perspective, there are dangers in this approach, not least that it takes a lot of time to build up this level of involvement. For individual policy projects, it requires a commitment to find the people who are willing to be involved and who have an interest in the issue, and to make sure that there is a representation across a range of interests. Inviting self-nominations runs the risk of being influenced by the most articulate or the best-funded lobby groups; inviting named individuals risks being seen to unduly lead the direction of the group, so there must be ways of reaching those people who are least likely to become involved in policy-making. This is likely to mean that groups will need strong facilitation and perhaps training in how to engage, particularly through technology, as well as thought about the best places and times to reach those who are disengaged.

There are risks too in the levels of transparency involved. Engaging the public at very early stages of policy development risks ridicule, accusations that the government does not know what it is doing, or it can lead people to believe that early thinking is nearer to the final decision and so they change their behaviour. Sometimes governments float policy ideas, particularly as we come towards elections, in order to see how the public responds. Some of those ideas are very quickly buried when it becomes clear that they are unpopular or unworkable, but they remain on public record for the party or the minister who proposed it and will be brought up repeatedly in years to come. Being willing to be transparent comes with personal and professional risk.

By exposing the thought processes of civil servants and ministers, it also risks leading them to self-censor in the early stages. Surprising as it may seem, some of the early ideas that come up are not very good, but in order to have good ideas it is often necessary to have many bad ideas, and to refine and build. There were many times during social partnership when final policies were not perfect but were enormously better than the original thinking, and in part this was possible because of the commitment to confidentiality that allowed participants to be brave enough to appear stupid in suggesting an idea.

Engaging the public also means being open to change. When citizens (and others) are involved only at late stages, the changes are likely to be small and at the level of detail. By involving them early, there is a risk that the thinking which underpins the proposal itself might change. This is a danger in a political system where parties have very different political ideologies, and where one party's ideology is dominant at any given time. Education policy based on individual responsibility to work hard and the belief that competition raises the performance of everyone will look different from policy based on a belief that it takes a community to raise a child.

Citizens' assemblies

Citizens' assemblies have been used in the UK, both locally and nationally. The UK Parliament commissioned its first citizens' assembly in 2018 to consider social care, while more recently, a Climate Assembly of 104 randomly selected people, representative of the UK population, met for six weekends in early 2020.

According to Involve,[6] an independent organisation that sets up and facilitates citizens' assemblies, there are three stages to an assembly process: learning, through a range of presentations from experts covering evidence and opinions; deliberation, where participants explore their own opinions and the opinions of others on what they have heard, and where experts can provide more clarification; and decision-making where the group comes to conclusions. Citizens' assemblies are not expected to come to a consensus, and there may be voting on different issues, so that minority views are heard and strength of feeling across issues can be understood by those who will make the final decisions. Decision-makers may also be present in the final stages, so that the participants can present their findings directly. The independent agency that facilitates has a responsibility to make sure that the evidence presented is factually accurate, comprehensive, balanced, and unbiased.

Clearly there are strengths to this kind of approach, particularly when it is high profile, as it can draw public attention to the issues and allow people to learn and understand the different opinions and experiences of those affected. It both brings decision-makers face-to-face with those who will be affected by their decisions and gives them an insight into public opinion based on an understanding of the evidence, and time to reflect on it. This gives a much better basis for decisions than opinions formed on social media or those of the most vocal and active groups.

Of course, running a citizens' assembly is a complex process, which requires time, money, and expertise in order to be successful. It must also lead to action or at the very least acknowledgement of the recommendations of the group; otherwise it will be seen as a publicity exercise and lead to greater mistrust of policy-makers. It is also vital that the problem to be explored does not have a preconceived outcome and that those in power are open to the idea that the assembly could come up with new ideas and solutions.

And perhaps this is why there are few representative deliberative processes used in developing education policy. The OECD suggests that representative deliberative processes are best used for issues that have a direct impact on people's everyday lives, that people have experience of, and on which people can form opinions. Although this sounds like a perfect fit for education issues, their research shows that urban planning, health, and the environment are the most likely to involve citizen representation across the different nations studied, and that education does not feature at all, unless as part of 'public services'.[7] The most recent list on Involve's 'Citizens Assembly Tracker' from July 2021 is almost exclusively focused on climate change.[8] It would be worth considering what broad education issues would suit a citizens' assembly model, perhaps beginning with the thorny question of the purposes of education.

This is something that the Irish Government has committed to, setting up a citizens' assembly on the future of education,[9] which will put those who are being educated at the centre. In setting up their citizens' assembly, the Irish Government understood that the 'hot topics' of the day, such as reforming the leaving certificate and supporting pupils with SEND, could only really be properly debated and taken forward in the context of answers to broader questions such as what education is for and how it can contribute to building a successful and sustainable society. They would also need to be open to learning about people's experiences of the education system and the values that underpin their understanding and opinions. Of course, framing the conversation around fundamental questions such as these can lead to interesting debate but no real conclusions, while framing it too narrowly risks polarising the debate, so developing the remit of the group, and the questions to be discussed, was a vital part of the process.

Those planning the citizens' assembly also discussed the challenges of really centring the voices of young people in the conversation, giving real weight to their views rather than taking a tokenistic approach. They were keen to ensure that conversation took place across Ireland to feed into the citizens' assembly discussions, rather than just in the citizens' assembly itself, recognising that these too would need to be facilitated. This process is being developed through an initiative called BEACONS (an unwieldy name that stands for Bringing Education Alive for our Communities on a National Scale),[10] run by the Irish Teaching Council (perhaps the equivalent of the Chartered College of Teaching or the General Teaching Councils of Wales, Scotland and Northern Ireland).

The idea of BEACONS is that it builds strong communities through developing conversations between teachers, parents, and students. It offers a forum for generating and discussing ideas that are important to the participants themselves. While the conversations happen at school level, part of the aim of the initiative is to find ways to link the bottom-up approach with national policy-making. In early evaluations of the model,[11] familiar problems emerged with ensuring diverse participation, making sure the voices of the 'seldom heard' were listened to, and responding to or acting on the ideas and issues generated. But participants were positive about the process and keen to engage further, and there was a strong desire to encourage feedback loops with the local community who were involved as well as to policy-makers at the centre.

Before we leap to adopt an Irish model of citizens' assemblies though, it is worth considering the views of those who think its praises may be overblown. David Farrell,[12] professor of politics at University College Dublin, who has advised governments in the UK, Ireland, and Belgium on citizens' assemblies, believes that the Irish model is too controlled by government, and worries that the recommendations and reports developed at great expense (both financial and in time) are not properly considered by the Oireachtas (the Irish Parliament). He suggests looking to Belgium, where agendas are developed by non-governmental bodies, and the Belgium Parliament is required to respond in full to the recommendations, with citizens' assembly members invited to debate with them. In February 2023, the Belgium Government became the first country to pass a law 'that allows deliberative committees to be formed and citizens' assemblies to be convened at the national level. These bodies are to advise the parliament on its political decisions'.[13] This law allows for sortition – a random sample of citizens is invited to apply to be part of a particular deliberative body, and then a second round of random selection from within those who apply ensures that the body will be representative of the population by gender, age, place of residence, and level of education. For Annelies Verlinden, Belgium Minister of the Interior, Institutional Reform, and Democratic Renewal, this is about 'making concrete work of citizen participation. Our ambition is to get citizens more involved in politics and give them insight into political decision-making. I am convinced that their insights can lead to more innovative ideas and that they can be an additional sounding board for Parliament'.[14]

Policy innovation and iteration

One of the difficulties of policy-making is that it is intended to bring about national and large-scale change, but it is difficult to know whether the proposed actions will be successful. Change is expensive and getting it wrong is costly financially, educationally, and in terms of the reputations of those who have made the decisions. At the same time, there is often a perceived moral driver to enact change quickly and in a widespread way. If you have an idea that you think will improve outcomes for children, improve teacher retention, or reduce inequality, why would you not be ambitious for everybody in the system and roll it out nationally, immediately?

We end up in an odd dichotomy, where policies need to be evidence-based in order to justify the effort and finances involved in enacting them – which can lead to repetition and painfully slow change – while at the same time some new ideas are forced through at rapid pace without the proper time to evaluate and improve

them. Both of these are unhelpful for supporting effective innovation and iteration, as evidence-based policy-making slips into policy-based evidence gathering.
As the saying goes, policy-makers 'use evidence like a drunk uses a lamppost, more
for support than illumination'.

Before looking at examples of different approaches in other countries, it is
worth noting the differential impact of two organisations in English education
policy: the Education Endowment Foundation (EEF) and the National Endowment for Science, Technology, and the Arts (NESTA). The EEF is designed to
bring the best evidence of what works in education to the system, with a deliberately high bar for demonstrating impact. It is part of the wider system of the
government-supported 'What Works Network' and has a preference for randomised controlled trials (RCTs) as the optimum way for showing how an intervention can lead to change.[15] This is positive in terms of the strength of evidence,
but it is also limited as there are only so many areas that have the robust data that
is convincing enough for the EEF, in part because of the aversion to undertake
trials that potentially advantage smaller groups for short periods of time. It is also
worth noting that the EEF has prioritised areas that resonate with the current
government – literacy (including phonics), numeracy, pupil premium – leaving
large areas of education policy untouched.

NESTA is a different beast, with a clearer legacy of supporting innovation, in part
to encourage creativity and talent, helping to support innovative ideas to come to
market. Its focus has shifted over the years, but it still retains a commitment to
forming a 'deep understanding of the problem at hand', 'relentlessly' prototyping
and discarding ideas until they find ones that work, borrowing ideas from different
fields and thinking differently.[16] They use data analytics, blend participatory practices with artificial intelligence, use the arts to influence behaviour and attitudes,
engage people in designing solutions, and use behavioural sciences to go beyond
changing individual behaviour to shaping systems. NESTA's 'Discovery Hub' is
central to challenging assumptions and looking to the future.

At present, the EEF is the dominant force in education policy-making, playing a
key role in determining the evidence base to be used for policies such as the Early
Career Framework and National Professional Qualifications. NESTA is not integrated into education policy-making to anything like the same degree. In England, policy-led evidence is trumping innovation approaches. How do other
countries do it differently?

One approach is the Policy Innovation Lab, which have become established in
many places. They are considered to be 'neutral organizations applying scientific,
lab-like methods to generate innovative, evidence-based policy solutions to complex social problems'.[17] While there is no agreed definition of 'policy innovation',
many of these labs place the user at the centre of policy development. They also
focus on building collaboration across organisations while providing space to
develop, build, and test different potential solutions. By providing the sorts of
skills and expertise that civil servants do not necessarily possess, they also help to
balance the tension between the risk-taking required for innovation and the
blame-avoidance tendencies at the heart of government.

There is no agreed structure for a policy lab. Many are established or commissioned by governments, based within the public sector but separate from it. They can be 'change agents' or 'hubs' that facilitate collaboration, collect evidence, and test ideas. They may also be 'ambassadors' for the policy lab methods, within their own commissioning organisation or beyond it.

Denmark's MindLab

Innovation labs exist in many places and grew out of the idea that the processes and mindsets needed for innovation are very different from those needed for stable policy-making and frontline delivery of services, and therefore very different from the skills that civil servants are expected to have traditionally. According to Carstensen and Bacon (who is a former Director of Innovation at MindLab),[18] an innovation lab helps in the exploration phase of policy-making, involving stakeholders and end-users in co-creation of policy, creating new solutions *with* people not just *for* people, which means they also help to support the implementation of policies and practices so developed. As they work, they evaluate their own processes and codify their own practices, so that they can be used by others or in other situations. 'At heart', they say, 'innovation labs are designed to foster collaboration.'[19] They do so by 'being permanent structures with a mission to temporarily unfreeze organisational embedded practices.'[20]

MindLab, established in Denmark in 2001, was one of the world's first public sector innovation labs, inaugurated in 2002 by the Ministry of Business Affairs. It started with five full-time staff, with skills in creative facilitation, team building, hosting, and policy development. It served two particular functions in the early stages, supporting civil servants to see that there were different ways of making policy that reached beyond writing papers while also contributing to project initiation meetings by mapping, visioning, and developing objectives.

By 2006, the new project-based policy development was reasonably well established across the ministry and so MindLab became much more a 'centre of excellence' focused on developing new initiatives involving businesses and citizens, supporting user-centred evaluations of current policies, and creating better methods for user-centred policy development. It also worked across three ministries, helping to break down institutional barriers and silos. It developed new ideas based on user needs, analysing those needs, testing ideas, and then evaluating the impact of the new action after it was implemented.

The staff hired by the new MindLab included those with skills in design, social research, and policy development. They were expected to understand the political process and how to work in the public sector. They were to focus on service and policy innovation, as well as its impact on users and on society. And they would work on 'wicked' social problems, those which were complex and unlikely to be solved. As it progressed, MindLab moved away from the 'centre of excellence' idea, introducing the concept of the laboratory where new ways of involving citizens were examined, and potential solutions trialled and developed. Carstensen and Bacon set out the seven phases of the process which MindLab codified as

'Project focus, learning about the users, analysis, idea and concept development, concept testing, the communication of results, and impact measurement'.[21]

In evaluating their activities, it became clear that MindLab was most successful when it was able to demonstrate to the decision-makers and change-makers across different departments what the world looked like to the end-users of their decisions, for example by explaining how it felt to be a young person navigating a complex tax system. This allowed ministry staff to change their focus and to understand their mission and purpose differently. They also understood that sustainable change could not happen through individual projects, but by 'deeper, longer-term, top-level engagement'.[22] This led to a focus on 'change partnerships' alongside a research strategy to develop findings on important new policy trends.

MindLab used ethnography and design methodology to engage citizens in designing solutions to problems. Staff not only conducted interviews, but observed what people actually do through techniques like video diaries or intermittent texting. They brought citizens, experts, and other stakeholders together to co-create ideas and design prototypes for rapid testing. They invited users to test these rough prototypes so that they could be adjusted or expanded.

MindLab was closed in 2018, replaced by a Digital Disruption Agency with a sharper focus on using digitisation to alter public sector priorities and performance,[23] but not before MindLab had developed a programme christened 'Lab Rats', which brought together people working for MindLab's partner organisations who would build on the ideas and innovations within their own organisations.

Singapore's Human Experience Lab

Singapore's 'Human Experience Lab' was set up in 2012, becoming officially known as the Innovation Lab in 2017. They began as a small design-thinking unit in the public sector division of Singapore's Prime Minister's Office. McKinsey reports on three of their initiatives, which show the policy lab processes at work.[24] In particular, the initiative to co-create solutions for people with disabilities started from the premise that the usual government methods of surveying do not unearth deep-seated issues or tensions. Instead, the team went to observe people with disabilities in their day-to-day lives, tapping into people's needs and aspirations and the barriers they encounter. They then brought together public servants, professionals in social services and healthcare, along with people with disabilities and caregivers to design solutions, and created a map of Singapore's social services infrastructure. This generated over 30 ideas, four of which went on to be implemented by different partners.

Futures thinking

Planning for the future is both difficult and divisive. As we have set out throughout the first half of this book, there are personal, organisational, and political constraints that limit the capacity to think longer term. In addition, there is the difficulty in making the imaginative leap needed to consider alternative possibilities for the future. Even radical reimaginings of education tend to start with the content rather than the mode of delivery – we still think about teachers standing in front of a class full of children, delivering content, something that proved inadequate when having to respond to the Covid-19 pandemic as the normal classroom dynamic became untenable for a time. The significant growth in the use of and interest in artificial intelligence (AI) has fuelled an industry around what it might mean for education, but what is most striking is how it tends to focus on existing systems and approaches rather than anything genuinely paradigm shifting. As the Joint Information Systems Committee (JISC) noted: 'It's worth considering what role the AI system is attempting to play in the teaching and learning experience. It might seem obvious that the aim is to support the teacher and this is the direction that is most often discussed. However, it could be argued that earlier attempts to use AI for education were actually trying to replicate or replace the teacher.'[25]

The other fertile debate for the future of education is around content – are we teaching children and adults the knowledge and skills they need to be successful in the future? As we have demonstrated in Chapter 2, this is a debate that has raged in the English context since the nineteenth century, most recently epitomised in the ongoing tussle between a knowledge-based curriculum (inspired by the Black Papers) and a skills-based curriculum (with its roots more firmly in the Plowden tradition). Given the ideology of the Conservative Government, it is no surprise that those challenging the traditional model of knowledge transmission and assessment are not getting traction (see, for example, NESTA's work in this area).[26]

The future is inevitable and unpredictable. We have to prepare for it, without knowing what it will be with certainty. We know it will look the same as the past until it does not, and we need to adjust. 'To achieve our vision and prepare our education systems for the future, we have to consider not just the changes that appear most probable but also the ones that we are not expecting.'[27]

What can we learn from international examples about how better to do this?

Scenario planning

A useful way to consider options for the future without divorcing from the past is through the lens of scenario planning, which allows the development of a small number of different possible future scenarios which can then be used to think about how to respond and what might be needed in a world where this kind of scenario is playing out, or how to prepare for or work to prevent particular types of scenarios. It is important to realise that this is not about predicting the future: the world is too complex and volatile for that to be either possible or desirable. Instead, those who develop scenarios consider current trends across a range of issues and try to extrapolate into a future where those trends are allowed to continue. This allows policymakers to consider the impacts of different possible futures and the potential impacts of policies. Considering a range of possible future scenarios also allows policy-makers to step outside their own disciplines to consider how different actions in other parts of the system might impact. This is much easier to see in looking to the future than when operating in the fast-paced, fast-changing present.

The OECD considered scenario planning in a 2020 report, 'Back to the Future of Education: Four OECD Scenarios for Schooling',[28] which suggested three distinct benefits from scenario planning: anticipation, policy innovation, and future-proofing. Developing a range of scenarios allows us to identify what is currently changing, which might not be obvious or which might have long-term impacts that are not immediately obvious. It enables us to find our own blind spots and to anticipate possibilities that are highly unlikely or do not appear particularly relevant, but which could catch us by surprise. Identifying these enables us to think about policies in a new way, giving us options for activities that might not seem the most intuitive in the present but which make sense in a world on the brink of change. It also allows us to future-proof current policies, testing them against different possible futures to understand some of the long-term consequences of current policies and proposals.

Scenarios can be helpful for a number of reasons, not least because they allow politicians and policy-makers to explore issues in an imagined future without laying blame or taking credit for the actions that led to that future. They allow experts to explore their own, and each other's, assumptions and biases in a way that opens up dialogue and learning possibilities, rather than in confrontational and divisive ways. By building narratives, it is possible to move beyond the facts and figures of policy-making and begin to feel what it might be like to live in these possible futures, to see them through different people's eyes, to see the bigger picture rather than zero in on particular pet issues. Some examples include the OECD's Andreas Schleicher thinking about future education scenarios for the World Economic Forum in 2021,[29] or the World Bank using scenario planning to help Romania consider responses to the Covid-19 pandemic.[30]

Integrated futures thinking

Scenario planning is a useful tool, but it still relies on a subject-specific lens (scenarios for education) and on building on our current understanding. What about the unexpected innovation, the area of change that sits outside of education policy but that can have a profound impact upon it? How do we use future thinking more broadly in policy-making?

In 2015, with the passing of 'The Wellbeing of Future Generations Act', Wales became the only country to impose duties to protect the needs of future generations. For its proponents, this is a way of making practical the scenario planning and futures thinking of other nations, of not only planning for possible futures but protecting the rights of people in the future by acting in the present. The Act also embeds the United Nations Sustainable Development Goals in Welsh law and policy-making. In the Act, the notion of wellbeing goes beyond the individual and refers to the state of the population. It is focused on improving four dimensions of wellbeing – the social, economic, environmental, and cultural – and is necessarily broad in scope. The Act applies to 44 public bodies including the Welsh Government, local authorities and health boards, national parks, and museums. It sets out seven national wellbeing goals, and requires public bodies to set objectives in line with the goals and show how they will work towards meeting them through their policies and practices. There are also five 'ways of working' that public bodies should use in meeting their objectives: long-term, prevention, integration, collaboration, and involvement.[31] These ways of working are vital to the way in which the Act is used, to put citizens at the heart of policies. In particular, decisions and actions taken by the public bodies concerned need to include a diverse range of those who are interested in achieving the goals; they need to be taken in collaboration with other organisations and individuals working for the same goals; and they need to integrate different areas of policy and practice rather than working in silos.

The Act also established the role of the Future Generations Commissioner, and a requirement to report to the Welsh Government every five years. The first report from the Future Generations Commissioner set out how the idea of looking to the future can help:

> Questions about the future have filtered into all aspects of our daily lives, forcing us to constantly re-evaluate and question what lies ahead. From automation, artificial intelligence, the fourth wave of the industrial revolution, the climate and nature emergencies, flooding, the outbreak of COVID-19, it is clear that these issues are not just for our scientists or philosophers to debate. These pose real dilemmas for those working in policy-making and public services.[32]

This first report sets out a range of trends 'to watch', including environmental, population and demographic, poverty and inequality, and technological, before exploring their potential impact specifically in the Welsh context. It goes beyond scenario building, because it then sets out a positive and aspirational vision of the future of Wales, in order to set out ways to build towards that future.

While Wales is the first country to legislate for future generations, the government in Finland has been producing a report on the future to the Eduskunta (Finnish Parliament) every five years since 1993. This report aims to identify issues that will be important for decision-making and policy-making during the parliamentary term.[33]

The Finnish 'Report on the Future' brings together systematic reflections on the future of Finland, carried out in a number of government ministries. Again, this is not about an attempt to predict the future but a way of opening up a number of possibilities, to challenge assumptions and to widen public understanding and awareness of the trends that will shape the future. The report contains four different scenarios, which are possible paths to the future, in order to reflect on how those paths might be influenced.

Several Finnish ministries carry out 'foresight' work, and there is also a joint foresight planning group which coordinates the work of those ministries. This group disseminates information and is the network to bring together the foresight work that will be part of the 'Report for the Future'.

In order to prepare a parliamentary response to the report, the Eduskunta has a Committee for the Future, a little like Westminster's Select Committees. This is made up of 17 members of the Eduskunta from across the political spectrum. While part of their role is to provide material for the Future report, they also make submissions to other committees about long-term issues, analyse research, and debate issues related to future development. At the beginning of each parliamentary session, the committee is given training in using and analysing futures methodology and understanding the research. A summary by the European Parliamentary Technology Assessment (EPTA) in 2013 likened the working of the committee to a think tank inside the Eduskunta, with a mission 'to conduct an active and initiative-generating dialogue with the government on major future problems and the means of solving them'.[34] It has been given the task of 'following and using the results of research' and its goal is to make policy.

Past reports have considered climate, the future of work, and wellbeing through sustainable growth. In developing the report for 2023, the government ran 50 dialogues on the future of Finland in different locations around the country, in order to hear from citizens whose voices would not normally be heard. This followed a government pledge to try out new ways of interacting in order to encourage people to be more involved in reforming society. This included a commitment to reaching people of different ages and genders, and from a variety of backgrounds. The government worked with a partner, TimeOut, and used a specific methodology to run the dialogues, which allowed every person to participate and to be heard. The methodology includes six ground rules: listening to each other, relating to each other and using everyday language, being open about experiences and how they might affect views, asking others directly about their views, being respectful and, importantly, bringing people together by finding the hidden and the unsaid and working through conflicts in an open manner. This allows participants to be heard and represented, but also enables them to listen to each other in order to understand better the perspectives from people they would not necessarily spend time with otherwise. These conversations, along with the foresight activity of the ministries, are brought together into the 'Report on the Future' for government and other policy-makers to reflect on.

Chapter summary

- It is important to seek lessons from international examples and other national jurisdictions.
- But we must be wary of a simplistic 'cut-and-paste' approach to importing policy-making ideas without understanding contextual factors.
- We can learn lessons in collaboration from countries that take a more comprehensive approach to citizen engagement, such as Estonia and Ireland.
- We can learn lessons in policy innovation from countries that have established and respected innovation approaches such as Denmark and Singapore.
- We can learn to think more clearly about the future and integrate future planning into the English policy-making cycle by learning lessons from the OECD, Wales, and Finland.

Notes

1 As part of early years reform proposals in 2012–14, civil servants brought together international comparisons for ministers to consider. As they did not seem to support the hoped-for agenda (cutting regulation), other countries were suggested, including Mugabe's Zimbabwe.

2 www.oecd.org/gov/open-government/innovative-citizen-participation-new-democratic-institutions-catching-the-deliberative-wave-highlights.pdf

3 www.opengovpartnership.org/stories/lessons-from-reformers-estonia-shifts-from-online-consultation-to-co-creation/

4 www.envir.ee/MAK2030#vabariigi-valitsusel (English translation)

5 Ibid.

6 www.involve.org.uk/resource/citizens-assembly

7 www.oecd.org/gov/open-government/innovative-citizen-participation-new-democratic-institutions-catching-the-deliberative-wave-highlights.pdf

8 https://involve.org.uk/citizens-assembly-tracker

9 https://irelandseducationyearbook.ie/downloads/IEYB2022/YB2022-Introduction-03.pdf

10 www.teachingcouncil.ie/news/teaching-council-welcomes-european-commission-and-oecd-study-on-school-community-engagement-in-ireland/

11 Ibid,

12 www.irishtimes.com/opinion/we-may-have-overdone-it-on-citizens-assemblies-1.4803375

13 www.buergerrat.de/en/news/way-clear-for-citizens-assemblies-in-belgium/

14 www.buergerrat.de/en/news/way-clear-for-citizens-assemblies-in-belgium/

15 www.gov.uk/guidance/what-works-network

16 www.nesta.org.uk/our-innovation-methods/

17 www.researchgate.net/publication/350964586_Policy_Innovation_Labs

18 www.innovation.cc/scholarly-style/2012_17_1_4_christian_bason_innovate-labs.pdf

19 Ibid.

20 Ibid.

21 Ibid.

22 Ibid.

23 Two former directors discuss the demise of MindLab in an interview here: https://apolitical.co/solution-articles/en/how-denmark-lost-its-mindlab-the-inside-story

24 www.mckinsey.com/~/media/McKinsey/Industries/Public%20Sector/Our%20Insights/How%20Singapore%20is%20harnessing%20design%20to%20transform%20government%20services/How-Singapore-is-harnessing-design-to-transform-government-services.pdf

25 https://repository.jisc.ac.uk/9232/1/ai-in-tertiary-education-a-summary-of-the-current-state-of-play-september-2023.pdf

26 www.nesta.org.uk/blog/reinventing-schools-future/?gclid=CjwKCAjwv-2pBhB-EiwAtsQZFGZnT92t11YvgNTfuAWYgxmHEIJCIGcQxTTLl2uuKgbUMTJrkQiOXBoCQSAQAvD_BwE

27 Andreas Schleicher, Director for the Directorate of Education and Skills, OECD, www.weforum.org/agenda/2021/01/future-of-education-4-scenarios/

28 www.oecd-ilibrary.org/sites/d08897ba-en/index.html?itemId=/content/component/d08897ba-en

29 www.weforum.org/agenda/2021/01/future-of-education-4-scenarios/

30 https://thedocs.worldbank.org/en/doc/470311603822962016-0090022020/original/EXPECTTHEUNEXPECTEDUsingScenarioPlanningforReopeningSchoolsinRomania.pdf

31 www.futuregenerations.wales/wp-content/uploads/2020/05/FGC-Report-English.pdf

32 Ibid.

33 https://vnk.fi/en/foresight/government-report-on-the-future

34 https://eptanetwork.org/static-html/comparative-table/countryreport/finland.html

6 What can we learn from different ways of thinking?

The approaches that we considered in Chapter 5 are underpinned by some specific ways of thinking. This chapter digs a little deeper into three of those: design thinking, systems thinking and relational policy-making. There are already organisations and groups using these approaches as they develop policy ideas, including groups within the civil service.[1] But while we could each point to some projects in which we were involved over the years which included some of these ideas, they are definitely not a major feature of policy-making in England.

This is necessarily a superficial overview of very complex ideas which academics and practitioners have spent many years exploring and explaining. It is intended to draw out some key ideas that we can build on as we develop our policy-making toolkit in the final three chapters.

Design thinking

Design has traditionally focused on creating beautiful and functional objects, but design thinking is increasingly being used to consider experiences, policies, careers, and lives.[2] It can be thought of as a range of tools, a way of solving problems and of challenging the way we think. IDEO, a global design company,[3] believes that design thinking is a human-centred approach, looking at the ways in which individuals and groups behave, how they use objects or services, how people interact in and between groups, and how that changes the ways in which they relate to the world and each other.[4]

Design thinking focuses on the person who will use the outcome and how they will use it. Key to this is empathy: understanding how others feel, think, and see the world. In designing a product, an experience, or a service, there is little point in making something perfect and beautiful that no-one will use. Imagine trying to design the lobby of a new hotel. A designer might have an idea for a different look: doric columns, cosy nooks, or clean lines. The lobby could look beautiful, but if it doesn't allow people to check in easily it will not be a good design.

Understanding how people check in to a hotel encourages designers to come up with ideas that will meet their needs. It is important not just to ask people what they want, or even what annoys them, but to observe them in different situations – when they're tired or distracted, when they are alone or in a crowd, when they have

DOI: 10.4324/9781032651057-7

luggage, when they're on a business trip or a holiday. These are the times when it becomes more obvious to the empathetic observer what 'work-arounds' people use.

It is probably helpful to work with 'extreme users' too – the people who travel all the time or those who stay in the same hotel every week for work, those who are on honeymoon or at a hen party. This may lead to decisions about who exactly an object is designed for, or at least an understanding that a single design may not work for every user.

The tools of design thinking include divergent thinking, generating as many ideas as possible; prototyping and trialling small parts of ideas along the way rather than waiting for the finished outcome; considering and using the experiences of 'ordinary people', experts, and 'extreme users', those who will use the design and those who will work in or with it. It is participative and collaborative. Ways of working may take us beyond the usual multidisciplinary team where everyone advocates for their own specialism and the outcome is the result of negotiation. Instead, it may focus more on interdisciplinary working, where ideas are collectively owned and everyone is responsible for them.

What are the benefits of design thinking?

Too often education policy ideas come from people whose experiences of education are from a long time ago, from a particular sort of education, and from a perspective (usually) of academic success. When policy-makers do decide to involve the people who will be impacted by their policy, their first stop is often some kind of survey, consultation, or (perhaps) a focus group, with questions set out from their limited perspective.

Design thinking puts those who will use the outcome at the heart of developing the outcome; it prompts designers to think about how the outcome will affect individual and group behaviour and how it will affect those with particular needs and behaviours outside the norm. Those who participate in developing the outcomes are more likely to use those outcomes and to extol the benefits to others. Encouraging large numbers of ideas, bringing together experts, outliers, and people with different knowledge and expertise, is likely to bring about innovative and exciting proposals, which can then be tried out in small ways to see what works where, while also encouraging more and better ideas to emerge.

How could design thinking be used in policy-making?

Ideally, design thinking would be part of the early stages of policy-making, in order to challenge the way we think about the issues to solve. Policy-making often skips this step, going directly to a definition of the problem that needs to be solved. By doing this, policies start in the wrong place and will end up being imposed on those who will implement them. For example, in April 2023, as teachers were striking over pay and funding, and the Department for Education missed its targets for teacher recruitment once again, Rishi Sunak (the UK Prime Minister) reiterated his proposal that all pupils in England should study maths until they're 18. He announced a review group – mathematicians, education experts, and business representatives – and their remit to offer advice on what should be taught and whether a new qualification for 16–18 year-olds is necessary. Predictably, the teacher unions and opposition parties pointed out the flaws: that there are not enough maths teachers, that it will take time and money to develop new qualifications, and that there are bigger problems to solve.

But let's assume for a moment that this is a policy worth designing. How might human-centred design change the way in which it could develop? It might begin by asking why many young people are leaving school without adequate skills, knowledge, and interest in maths. It would do this not by asking mathematicians or business representatives, or even teachers and pupils, but by observing what happens. Henry Ford is quoted as suggesting that if people had been asked at the turn of the twentieth century what would make their travel better, they would have suggested faster horses, and just asking questions about maths is likely to lead to similarly limited ideas. But by observing how teachers teach and learners learn, the impact of curriculum and assessments, and how young people use maths in their daily lives and jobs, a range of different problems are likely to emerge, particularly if these observations take place across the age ranges.

This is not about observing perfectly planned and executed 'Ofsted-ready' lessons, but about seeing what happens in a secondary classroom at the end of the Autumn term, watching how pupils engage with their learning and how everyone deals with disruptions. What are the routines that teachers and pupils fall back on when they're tired or distracted? Starting from a place of empathy is more likely to end up with policy designed to solve the problems that people are facing.

Design thinking would bring policy-makers, teachers, and pupils together to discuss the observations, as well as exploring the thinking of those affected by current policies and who would be affected by changes. It would include 'extreme users' – pupils with special educational needs, special schools, and pupil referral units – along with a range of experts and ordinary people – pupils who love maths and those who hate it, teachers who are qualified to teach maths and those who are not. Of course, the ideas that come up are unlikely to be limited to what should happen in maths at 16–18, but will range across different subjects and year groups, different school activities, relationships with employers, careers advisers, and youth workers. Ideas would spark new ideas, and those who were involved would be energised by this divergent thinking.

With skilled facilitation, the ideas would begin to converge. Themes would emerge, ideas that are more suited to the school day and structure. These are the ideas that would be taken forward by the design group, although some of the other ideas might easily be taken forward elsewhere – by employers or youth organisations, for example. Then comes the prototyping.

When designing an object, it is easy to see how a prototype might be built cheaply and offered to many users to see what the issues might be. But prototypes do not have to be tangible objects; they can be storyboards, role play, or computer simulations. Design thinking requires many prototypes, and early: a small idea, a curriculum thread, trialled by a single teacher; a curriculum unit, used in a small group of schools; a computer assessment, a workplace project, any number of ideas developed in a small way with the intention of seeing what happens. This allows very particular things to be evaluated: what training would a teacher need in order to teach this? How would this fit within the current curriculum? Does it make sense in a special school...? Designs can be changed and new ideas developed, depending on how the prototypes fare.

Policy-makers could be part of this process, sitting alongside those who were trying things out. It might prompt them to consider broader questions about links between a post-16 maths requirement and earlier curriculum stages, about careers guidance, work experience, or extracurricular activities. They would hear first hand what is needed to free up curriculum space for these new ideas. And they might begin to understand how much detail is needed in this new curriculum, how much can be left to teachers to design, and what sort of accountability measures are needed. To be truly empathetic, designers and policy-makers need to do their best to leave behind their assumptions and biases.

What are the risks of using design thinking for policy-making?

The openness of the design process is both part of its attraction and a key risk: policies that emerge may not be the same as those originally announced by ministers. They may not be as neat as a new curriculum and a new qualification. They may involve new relationships between schools and others, new thinking about accountability and assessment. They may challenge the structures and systems in place. This is a big challenge for a process that currently consults people once ideas are quite well developed, where civil servants spend very little time observing the people they design policies for, and where knowledge and experience that doesn't fit the model can be too easily disparaged or discarded.

It may also not solve the problem you set out to solve. In working empathetically with the users, it is possible that new problems will be identified that are more urgent or where solutions may have more impact. It may be that the problem identified has many different drivers and that its solution will have to be complex and multi-faceted. This could lead to ideas that require change across a large number of processes and that will seem too hard and too time-consuming. The problem is of course that any policy solution, however derived, is likely to require change across more areas than just the one it seeks to resolve, but that by working in isolation policy-makers can ignore those areas that are outside their remit, leading to 'unintended' but perhaps easily predicted consequences.

Design thinking, particularly in its divergent thinking phase, will come up with a vast number of ideas. Almost all of these will be impractical in a large-scale system, will have flaws that render them impossible to use, or just will not work. The risk is that too much time can be spent making suggestions when what is needed is a decision. Participants may become frustrated with the process because ideas are not acted on quickly, change is too slow. Policy-makers who are used to considering a small number of ideas will find it difficult to know how to decide between them. And politicians who want to announce the next big policy decision will find it hard to wait.

Linked with this is the fact that many of these ideas will not work because of other constraining factors. The Treasury limits the decisions that ministers can make because of limited resources made available to departments. Some ideas may require more teachers, more curriculum time, or more space in schools; others may require more support from other professionals. There are clear links between education decisions and those made in employment, benefits, and social services policies. And politicians are constrained by their need to be elected and to have favourable press coverage. Because design thinking happens on the ground, in the classroom, those who come up with the ideas may have no idea of these constraints. This of course is the opposite problem to that we currently have, where those who come up with the ideas have little idea of the constraints of the classroom or the workplace.

The other obvious risk to policy-making is that design thinking takes a lot of time. Sending civil servants into schools for long periods of observation, bringing teachers and others together to discuss and learn, coming up with ideas and then trying them out, rethinking and retrialling – all of these things take time and we know that teachers and civil servants are already stretched. Of course, we are using an old view of policy-making to judge a new model. These activities take time, but for teachers could be part of a strong culture of professional development. Many teachers are desperate to take time out to reflect on their practice, to have opportunities to observe and be observed non-judgementally, to talk about how their teaching, pupil learning, and 'the system' can be improved. Many use their own time and money to gain doctorates, to become Chartered Teachers, to study abroad. They join union working parties, take part in activities within their subject associations. Design thinking can help teachers to use their professional development time more effectively to make change beyond their own classrooms or their own schools.

Of course, the current model of policy-making takes time as well, particularly at the end of the process when teachers have to be trained to use the new process and have to change their curriculum or resources or pedagogy to fit the new policy. This time is rarely factored into policy-making.

Another risk is the time it can take to make serious change. Governments like fast change, to be able to make a proposal and to see it through within a political term, and there is always the argument that children only have one shot at education so that if we know something 'works' we should implement it immediately. The risk of taking a long time to bring about change is that some children will miss out. In the current policy-making system of course the risk is that changes are implemented quickly and the negative consequences take time to become apparent. Quick changes may lead to poor outcomes for particular groups of children, or impact on the breadth of the curriculum or on the retention of good teachers, but by the time we realise this, the policy has become embedded and new policies will have to be developed in order to rectify the problems. Any large-scale policy change is an experiment with children's lives and, however well it is trialled and evaluated, it can take a long time to see the impacts, large or small, positive or negative.

Alongside this is the idea that prototyping is included in design thinking – a large number of 'experiments', many of which won't work. This is deemed unfair to those children who take part in 'failed' experiments, as well as to those who miss out on activities that 'work'. But we have become used to the idea of randomised controlled trials, which measure the outcomes of clearly defined interventions against the attainment of similar groups without the intervention. Agencies pilot exam questions and SATs papers. And we pilot or trial national policies – an Ofsted framework or a baseline assessment – although this is usually at a stage when the decisions to make are about how to implement it well.

As an example, baseline assessment has been through a number of different iterations, each of which could be thought of as experiments. In its first appearance, in the late 1990s, it took the form of a large number of different assessments, developed mainly by local authorities, which were nationally accredited for school use. This form lasted until around 2001 when the Foundation Stage was introduced. More recently, the Department for Education spent a large amount of money trialling three different assessments before deciding that they would not work. Finally (for now), it gave more money to NFER to develop the current baseline assessment, invited schools to trial it, and then rolled it out to everyone. The danger of these 'experiments' is that nobody quite knows what success looks like and when the next trial will come along.

The sort of trialling and prototyping that takes place in design thinking is small scale and quick. There are already organisations that work like this, developing ideas in assessment and digital report cards,[5] for example. These are low stakes, initially involving a small number of participants trying out a number of ideas, discarding and reshaping as they go along, trying out different parts of an idea, or trying it with different groups. Ideas that don't work provide an opportunity to learn quickly and move on rather than requiring a high-stakes U-turn. In education, surely more than anywhere else, we should be able to reconceptualise failure as the best way to learn.

Systems thinking

Systems thinking is a way of looking at the world that takes in patterns and structures as well as individual parts. It acknowledges the complexity of relationships between parts of the system, as well as the impact of our own activity within the system. Peter Senge, in *The Fifth Discipline*, [6] talks about looking through complexity to the underlying structures. Systems thinking reminds us that changes have an impact on different parts of the system, not all of them immediately obvious. More than a process, systems thinking is about relationships and interactions between processes and people.

While systems thinking is often a feature of working with technology, it can also be understood through the lens of ecosystems. As one aspect of an ecosystem changes, it can have effects all around the system, often in totally unexpected ways. For example, the decline in bees and other pollinating insects can be linked to habitat destruction and pesticide uses, and has huge unintended and unpredicted consequences for food production. But in the almond-producing regions of California, trying to solve the problem by shipping in honeybees has done more harm to the already-endangered native bee population, as well as introducing disease into the honeybee colonies. Many believe that it is the large-scale agricultural systems themselves that need to change.[7]

Because systems thinking looks at the big picture, it does not assume that a problem has a single cause or a single solution. Those trying to solve a complex issue are encouraged to come up with a range of hypotheses both about the causes and the solutions. With its focus on interconnectedness, it is less likely to discount the 'difficult' or 'strange' data that doesn't fit the hypothesis: understanding, for example, how hormones affect different medicines comes from studying the effect of drugs on women at different ages and stages of the reproductive cycle, rather than discounting them because their hormones 'interfere' with the data. It can also be used at many different levels of problem-solving, whether that is about an individual, a team, a department, or an organisation – in fact, it can sometimes be helpful to cycle through the different 'levels' in order to challenge thinking.

Systems thinking is not about controlling the system or even about predicting what will happen. But it does mean that different proposals can be more comprehensively worked through, so that the possible consequences in unexpected parts of the system can be understood. Consequences are not unintended if they have been anticipated but still allowed to happen.

Systems thinking requires a number of fundamental shifts to be made in our thinking.

We need to see systems as circular rather than linear. In some very simple systems, an action will have a defined and consistent output, but in environmental, economic, workplace, and educational systems – as well as many others – input does not lead to output in a straightforward way. Everything is interconnected, reliant on other parts of the system in order to survive or to grow.

That complexity cannot be contained or controlled. Instead, we have to begin by trying to understand how the system works, how its parts interact. This is best done by talking to people inside the system, by observing the system at work, and by doing these things with an open mind. We are often part of the system we're studying, and our assumptions will colour the way we perceive it, so being able to surface and acknowledge those assumptions and to hold them lightly is key to this learning. Studying the system in this way also lets us ask how we got here, what behaviours have influenced the way the system works, and allows us to project those behaviours into the future to ask what will happen if we continue with them. This is very different from the model of starting by asking what is wrong with a system and then defining the problem by its solution, leading to narrow 'solutions' and stopping us from seeing the effective behaviours already present elsewhere in the system.

Systems thinking means thinking about the whole system, instead of breaking it down into parts. Analytic thinking isolates the parts of a system and studies each part individually. Systems thinking understands that the system is bigger than its component parts, and that it is a function of the relationships between the parts and the players within them. Analysis is part of the mechanical mindset but, by breaking the system down and making changes in one part, we don't take the connectedness of the system into account and will miss the impact of changes in other parts of the system. Of course, as soon as you begin to look at 'the system', it becomes clear that it is bigger than first assumed and that it both includes and is part of many other systems. Studying the interconnections allows a systems thinker to see both the big picture and the component parts.

Because of this interconnectedness, there is constant feedback. Actions in the system reinforce each other, positively or negatively. This could be a 'snowball effect', where outcomes of an action keep getting bigger, or a 'Pygmalion effect' where assumptions, good or bad, affect the outcome. Alternatively, feedback can be balancing, where a system self-corrects in order to meet the goals set. This is why, so often, the status quo in an organisation is maintained even when everyone actually wants change. An employer can continually talk about reducing the hours employees work, but without considering the numbers of projects the company is engaged in, or the ways in which projects are allocated, those hours will continue to increase.

Understanding feedback is about understanding causes and effects, the influences on a system. Because systems are complex, these are often not straightforward, linear relationships, but trends and patterns. Causes can have effects that take a long time or have different consequences over time; something that has an immediate positive effect can also be having indiscernible negative effects that compound and show up later. Or they can have different effects across different parts of the system, leading to those 'unintended' and sometimes 'perverse' consequences. Delays in feedback can mean that it takes time for a system to reach a balance: the more aggressively you make a change, the longer it can take to reach the desired outcomes. The bias towards action (see Chapter 1) can mean that we want to add new activities instead of removing barriers. Sometimes policy-making is about treating the symptoms rather than the problem itself, and treating the symptoms can stop us from looking at the underlying factors.

What is key to systems thinking is mapping all the 'things' that are part of the system and the ways in which they relate to each other. This can make the patterns clearer, the ways in which relationships influence the different parts, the places where feedback loops happen, and can lead to more and better ideas of the best places to intervene to make changes.

How does this relate to education policy-making?

Everybody understands that education is a system. The education system includes pupils, those who work in schools and colleges, and the institutions themselves. It includes the organisations that work around schools, inspection agencies, exam boards and testing agencies, those who train teachers, and those who provide resources. It includes government departments and ministers. However, too often the way in which policy is made is through breaking the system down into parts and manipulating them in isolation.

Within the education system, many of those component parts are also systems: individual schools, curricula, assessment, accountability, teacher training and development, the list goes on. It is also a system that sits within broader systems: employment and skills, the economy, health, welfare. Early years, primary, secondary, and further and higher education all sit within slightly different systems, contain different systems, and are all within the education system. Policy-making is also part of the system and a key component that influences the system.

We all have our own ideas about how the education system operates, where the difficulties are, and what the levers are that could bring about change. We may believe that excessive workload is caused by government bureaucracy, accountability and inspection systems, the demands of headteachers, and the needs of children. Each of these may be true, in part. By surfacing our mental models of how these issues 'cause' workload, drawing diagrams of how they interact, we will broaden our thinking about the whole system. Still, none of this will be a perfect answer.

Why don't policy-makers think in systems?

Systems thinking takes time, while politics – and education policy – seems to demand quick answers. But more than this, unpicking and mapping the education system shows how complex it is and how many interlocking parts it has. Every action will have consequences across a range of different processes and there is a danger that by trying to map every single one no action is ever taken. Most parts of the broader 'system' is outside the remit of the Department for Education (see Chapter 3). Systems thinking could lead to questioning how much benefit change will have when there are so many moving parts.

It is very hard to think beyond a specific problem that needs to be solved. Ministers and others in positions of power have a particular brief and often their own strong ideas for what needs to change. A laser focus on the particular issue, whether it is phonics teaching or academisation, can lead to enormous change in that issue, but it is extremely difficult to see or to acknowledge the things that are happening beyond it. The Department for Education itself creates boundaries, and those within it may find it difficult to see how their position interacts with other parts of government, or indeed how it interacts with schools and teachers.

Within the policy-making system, it is too easy to see failures as the responsibility of others. This is particularly the case with the split between policy-making and implementation. When policies go wrong, it is easy to point to the ways in which it was implemented – teachers who did not believe in the policy, rules that were too easily misinterpreted. We see this in Ofsted's 'myth-busting' – the need to constantly explain practices that are 'not required' by Ofsted, even though some of those practices were previously part of the inspection process. It is too easy to blame headteachers for continuing to demand seating plans or detailed lesson planning 'because Ofsted will want to see it', rather than looking at why such perceptions exist in order to understand the changes that could be made within the system.

In making changes, people are often reactive, fighting 'the enemy' rather than looking at their own contributions to the system. Continuing the Ofsted theme, while many people find the inspection regime and particularly its single-word judgements abhorrent and unhelpful, many schools still display banners that proclaim them to be 'Outstanding', their letterheads celebrate their Ofsted judgement, and heads and MAT leaders take to X (formerly Twitter) to celebrate the hard work that has gone into a 'successful' Ofsted inspection outcome.

It is also too easy to react to the immediate, to crack down on increased pupil absence by setting policies that threaten to fine and imprison parents, or to react to downward movement in international league tables by doubling down on the curriculum, its teaching, and its testing. This stops us from taking time to look for the gradual processes that led to the changes and can lead to addressing the wrong question, or making changes that have unforeseen impacts elsewhere or that swing the pendulum more violently in the opposite direction. Systems thinking shows the dangers of rapid interventions. Many problems show up a long time after the event that caused the problem; others grow exponentially so that a small problem stays small and under the radar until just before it becomes a big problem. The classic example is a pond where lily leaves double every day. Growth can seem small and manageable, and then the pond is completely covered with lily leaves just one day after it was only half covered. Teacher workload which grows exponentially can seem like a small problem, an individual problem, for a long time until it becomes a huge problem seemingly overnight.

But systems thinking also requires questioning power dynamics. Systems are made up of people, and people do not do things in predictable patterns. Understanding systems means accepting this reality rather than trying to change it.

Relational policy-making

Policy is intended to have an impact on people, on those who are the 'target' of policy and those who will implement it. In many cases, there are also people who will be indirectly affected by policy change. All of these people are in relationship, with each other and with 'the state' or other entity that is creating policy. Relational policy-making is a way of taking these relationships into account. It can also be aimed at creating, maintaining, or strengthening these relationships, and sometimes at disrupting them.

According to Bartels and Turnbull (2019),[8] a relational approach moves away from the notion of the state 'delivering' services to people, towards a system of co-production of services with the people who use them and those who provide them. It involves the state actively creating conditions for citizens to relate to each other, in consciously building better civil society. This is a long way from the political model in which we are currently operating, where politicians and the media emphasise the differences between people: the migrants with 'different values'; the poor who 'refuse to work'.

At its best it is about more even than focusing on building relationships. In its similarities with relational pedagogy,[9] it is about understanding that the perspectives of the marginalised, the outliers, the 'different' are vital to building society. It is not 'learning about' different perspectives, but about those being woven into the fabric of society. In school terms, it is about building education so that it includes everyone, rather than creating a system that works for most children and then thinking about the extra support that needs to be added so that children with SEND can access it too.

What would this mean for education policy?

It could be argued that government already operates some kind of relational policy-making. After all, there is plenty of engagement with teachers, through working parties and commissions which involve school staff, and through surveys and inquiries to which everyone can respond. And there are regular meetings with unions, currently through the 'Programme of Talks', previously through social partnership, along with opportunities for 'bilaterals' – meetings between civil servants or ministers and a single union. Ministers speak at conferences and events where teachers will be present, and there have been times when ministers have been willing to meet small groups of union members at annual conferences or Executive Meetings and listen to their concerns.

Because of the way in which policy ideas are developed, most of these engagements come too late in the process to be truly relational. Ministers and the department have too often already come up with both the problem to be resolved and the intended solution. These may have been signalled in party manifestos or in Green or White Papers. The best that the profession can hope for is an opportunity to shape the policy so that it might work. Of course, politicians do not come up with their ideas in a vacuum, and they may well have consulted with experts in education and read many books: Nick Gibb is well known for his reverence for the academic E.D. Hirsch,[10] and will often quote him. They will learn from and contribute to the work of think tanks and unions (for those on the left at least). But this is part of the problem. As we saw in Chapter 2, these relationships are usually with those experts who chime with the values and ideas of the minister or the party, who will form the working parties, commissions, and expert groups. Ideas and advice from the unions are more or less tolerated, depending on the political persuasion of the policy-makers, but are mostly sought once the ideas have been firmed up. And when ministers speak at conferences, and even when they engage in conversations with teachers, it is much more likely to be about selling a policy, perhaps hearing about some of the practical problems that may arise when it is implemented, than about truly developing relationships with those who will implement or be impacted by the policy.

If relational policy-making is to co-produce policies, and also to build relationships, there needs to be a fundamental shift in how policy is made. To begin with, there needs to be opportunities for real listening between all the parties involved. Policy-makers need to understand the realities of the lives of those who are impacted by the policies they make. Teachers need to understand how policies are made, how political priorities are determined, the limits within which policy-makers operate. And there needs to be transparency and respect for the beliefs and experiences of each person in the process.

What is the difference between relational policy-making and stakeholder engagement?

Policy-makers would argue that they are always building relationships, and that is true. But relational policy-making requires a different mindset from the stakeholder engagement that is usually the extent of this relationship building. The purpose of relational policy-making is not to persuade, to sell, or to manage expectations: it is to develop relationships, and not just between the policy-makers and the stakeholders. This kind of policy-making is about building relationships between those who will be impacted by policies, between them and those who will implement policy. The point is to improve those relationships as well as to change practice, and ultimately to build a more caring, more open society instead of pitting people against each other.

Stakeholder engagement usually happens after proposals have been set out and sometimes after decisions have been made. The point then is to give opportunities for stakeholders to provide feedback on the ideas. Good engagement will lead to the policy-makers having a better understanding of the problems that will need to be overcome, the ways in which the implementation of policy might go awry, and therefore how it could be done better. It will give an understanding of the people who are most likely to support and those who will object, and allow for more thought to be given to how to win over the doubters or how to use the supporters to build more enthusiasm. It gives policy-makers the opportunity to explain the benefits of the decisions, to show how it will make things better, and perhaps to demonstrate the thinking that has gone into making the decisions, to show why other ideas would not have met the aims or would not have been possible. Stakeholders may have the opportunity to tweak the edges, to offer suggestions for how things could be better. As an example, during the work to introduce a new national curriculum, conversations with the unions led to an additional Inset Day being made available so that there was a little more time for teachers to plan. But none of these engagements offer opportunities for policy-makers to understand the realities of life in the classroom; none allow teachers, parents, and policy-makers to sit together and really listen to each other's concerns and to try to build something that would work for everyone. None offer the chance for teachers of children with special needs to sit with parents of those children alongside policy-makers and for each of those groups to hear the ideas and the fears of the others.

Stakeholder engagement often stops once the policy has been announced. Policy-makers need to move on to building the next policies. The onus for implementing, perhaps months or years down the line, falls to the stakeholders. The responsibility for working out how this policy can fit within current work sits with the stakeholders. The difficult task of finding the time to learn, to change practice, to understand the impacts, and to manage the reactions of others falls to stakeholders within their already busy and fraught working lives.

Relational policy-making is an attempt to co-design policy and work towards co-implementation. It requires, as far as possible, a non-hierarchical framework, or at least one where every group's expertise and boundaries are acknowledged. Of course, government holds the purse strings, and has the overview (perhaps) of other policies, other concerns that need to be addressed nationally. Teachers hold expertise in their practice, their knowledge of their subjects and of how children learn and develop. Employers understand what they need to be profitable, and what skills and attitudes they need from their employees. Parents know their own children. The point of building these relationships is not for each group to be able to develop that same expertise. It is not to change the beliefs or assumptions of the others. But it is to build understanding, and to build policy – and education – that includes all perspectives.

What is required for relational policy-making to work?

If policy-making is to become more than stakeholder engagement, stakeholders need to become involved in the process from earlier stages and at deeper and more active levels. There are of course different levels at which practitioners can become engaged in policy.

Moreland-Russell et al. (2016) explored this from the perspective of public health policy in the USA,[11] setting out a range of skills and experience needed for practitioners to be at the heart of policy-making and to have real influence. To be engaged at any deep level, practitioners need the skills to identify the problems that need to be addressed. In education terms, teachers know well the issues in their own classrooms, and often across their schools. The skill is to be able to extrapolate from those issues, to use data and research to understand this as a wider issue. In union committees, in working groups, and through consultations, teachers are often very good at explaining how this issue impacts the children they teach and comparing notes with other teachers, but spend less time accessing and understanding the data across the system. This is not the fault of teachers: the system is organised in such a way that there is little time to look up from the individual classroom issues and to see the system as a whole.

Once an issue has been identified, practitioners need to be able to identify strategies to address it. Again, teachers are exceptional at this within their own classrooms; school leaders can do this across their schools. A behaviour issue may be related to an individual child and their circumstances, but by having conversations with other colleagues it may turn out that this is more of an issue of how the classroom is managed, an issue with the timetable or the structure of the school day. These are then issues that can be addressed school wide. But it is possible, when teachers have the time to engage more deeply with others that they see that the problem is about more than their children or their school. This could be an issue of poverty or hunger, of mental health, of lack of teaching assistants or pastoral work. Engaging with young people and their families may highlight despair at the lack of obvious opportunities beyond school, a lack of parental understanding of the way schools operate. The point is that only by having the time and opportunity to build relationships, and the skill to work with others, can teachers begin to develop possible solutions that go beyond their own practice.

Of course, once the issue and some possible strategies have been identified, practitioners need to be able to take others with them, to identify those who have the power to make change and to work out how to influence them. This requires an understanding of the policy process: the role of government, both local and national, the significance of Green and White Papers, and the role of Select Committees, Westminster Hall debates, and Parliamentary Questions, for example. Practitioners need an overview of the policies under which they currently operate, and how those affect their daily work. And they need to know who the people are who are influential.

Having influence does not necessarily happen directly. It is possible to lobby ministers, to engage with your MP, to attend local council education committee meetings, or to meet with officials. But it is also likely that there are other people, other groups who have influence with the decision-makers. There are also good times to influence, particularly around local or national elections. There is a skill to understanding who has influence, the people to whom the decision-makers listen. There is a skill to building a range of different ways of influencing, bringing diverse groups of people together with multiple perspectives. This is in part how unions and education campaigners work.

Policy is not always, and perhaps not often, changed because of facts and figures. It is important to have the data, but most people are more often swayed by stories, by finding shared values, and by their feelings that something is wrong. The evidence, including the numbers, is important to back up the feelings. Teachers are well placed to tell the stories, to make the issue personal to a child, a young person, a family. The skill is to find the balance between stories and data, between feelings and facts.

What are the problems with relational policy-making?

This kind of engagement in policy-making is of course time-consuming. For teachers to build positive relationships, let alone to carry out their own reflection and come up with ideas for solutions, means taking time away from the classroom and away from the work needed to support their teaching. Teachers are already working very long hours, with little time for professional development that supports and improves their teaching practice, so taking time out for policy work is likely to come much further down the priority list. We find this in union work: those teachers who have time to engage have often found ways to step away from the classroom. This can lead to those teachers who take part in union deliberations being further from the classroom than their colleagues, and perhaps being closer to members in difficulty and to the more problematic parts of education than to the day-to-day work of teachers.

Unions try to work around these difficulties by holding meetings on Saturdays or having conferences during Easter or bank holiday weekends, but this requires other sacrifices for members of family- or leisure time. This leads to the engagement of members who can take time away from families, which often rules out those with young children, or those caring for children or adults with health or other needs. Policy deliberations are stronger when they include diverse perspectives.

These problems are even greater when trying to build relationships with parents, who may not be particularly clear about why they should try to influence education policy. Even where parents can see a real need to change policy, traditional policy-making has a 'them and us' feel to it, so that it can feel like a battle. This is particularly true for parents of children with special needs, who often begin by battling a system that does not work for their child and end up using their hard-won skills to battle to make the system fairer for everyone.

Relational policy-making is not a quick win for politicians either. If the main point of this work is the building of relationships, time for that needs to be factored in. It is not a case of making arguments that seem popular with voters and then working out ways to bring those about. It is quite likely that policy ideas will change as participants build relationships and really understand what is needed. There is a 'them and us' feel to policy-making for education staff too, particularly if there is a conflict of ideology or of fundamental values. Teachers have not forgotten that Michael Gove as Education Secretary suggested that they, and their unions, were part of a left-wing Blob, and the Conservative Party has long believed that university education departments harbour dangerous socialist ideas. Equally, there are plenty of teachers who are worried that a Labour Government would undo much of the 'rigour' of the current system and move away from strong traditional education principles. Although everyone in education wants to see children and young people succeed, there are many disagreements about what success looks like and how it is measured. There are disagreements about the factors that contribute to success. And ultimately, there are power imbalances – between government and education staff, between teachers and parents, between employers and young people – which all need to be navigated in real relationship building.

This kind of policy-making requires real trust between all players. This does not build up overnight. In the current climate, there is a very long way to go before teachers trust politicians with the education system; there is a long way to go before parents and students trust that there is a real desire for equity or for the support that many need in order to have any chance of succeeding. The unions have been too easily split, whether between the different unions or within their own ranks. Too often, union members are accused of being political, or factional, and they are pitted against pupils and families. Unfortunately, there is also a lack of trust between education staff themselves, with the divisive arguments about knowledge and skills, between silent corridors and restorative justice policies, between traditional and progressive, academic and vocational, leading to a lot of belittling and unhelpful social media.

Why is relational policy-making a good thing?

Policy-making that begins with the people it impacts is more likely to work than policies developed without an understanding of the realities of the classroom. Listening to people who are deeply engaged in the system, whether as teachers, parents, inspectors, academics, or employers, can also make those people feel more involved in the policies that are developed and therefore have more of a stake in their success. Unfortunately, this does not happen in every instance, and engagement that does not lead to meaningful changes in policy leads very quickly to feelings of powerlessness at best and cynicism at worst. Relational policy-making goes further, focusing as it does on building relationships between policy-makers and stakeholders and between the stakeholders themselves, and prioritising transparency, openness, and trust. While not every problem identified in a relational policy-making situation can be solved, and not every proposed solution will be viable, those engaged in the process will understand better the reasons why. Involvement in the process will have shown how different players have been open to change, not through negotiation and compromise, but because ideas have been genuinely considered. This is far more likely to lead to policies which will succeed because everyone truly has a stake in their success. It will also lead to an openness to iterative policy-making, the possibility that changes can be made to suit different contexts while maintaining fidelity to the policy, because players really understand the purposes and the reasons for the policy.

Positive relationships between those who work for the good of education are also an important source of resilience. Too often, we think of resilience as an individual attribute of people who can pick themselves up after a setback or who can plough on regardless, meaning that it is easy to lambast those who struggle with high workloads or difficult pupil behaviour instead of working to make the system better for all. People become more resilient not by self-improvement but by things like being part of a community,[12] taking part in professional development, having agency, and feeling heard. All of these things are part of the focus of relational policy-making.

This is not just true for teachers and education staff. Pupils and their families can become more resilient and more motivated by being involved in communities where they are heard and where their knowledge and expertise is valued. In relational pedagogy,[13] it is clear that the relationships that are valued are not those where everyone agrees with each other, where everyone says the same things and has the same values. Instead, the value comes in teachers having the time to truly listen to the lived experiences of pupils and their families, and to recognise how the values of different communities may not be reflected in schools in the same way. And in families, students, and teachers working together to shape values that are reflective. This can lead to a much greater cooperation between families and schools.

These three different ways of thinking – design, systems, and relational – each have clear possibilities for improving the ways in which we make education policy. It is also clear that they feel a long way from our current policy-making system, and there are many who would call us naive to suggest that we could begin to operate in these ways. But we think these ideas are helpful prompts to think about how we could engage more people at early stages of policy thinking, evaluate ideas earlier in the process, and consider how our actions might impact on different parts of the system and over time.

Chapter summary

- This is a brief and superficial overview of three big approaches to policy thinking, pulling out some key themes that will help to build our toolkit.

- Design thinking considers human-centred design as a broad way of engaging with policy-making and a range of tools, including divergent thinking, prototyping, and 'user engagement'.
- Systems thinking sees how considering education as a system of processes and relationships helps to explain the complex effects policy can have on different parts of the system and over time.
- Relational policy-making goes deeper into the idea of building relationships in order to improve policy and ultimately to improve education.

Notes

1 See, for example, this blog series from the UK Government's 'multidisciplinary policy design community', https://publicpolicydesign.blog.gov.uk/about-this-blog/ or the 2016 Open Policy Making Toolkit from the Cabinet Office.
2 Many of the ideas in this section come from Tim Brown, with Barry Katz, *Change by Design: How Design Thinking Transforms Organizations and Inspires Innovation* (HarperCollins, 2009).
3 www.ideo.com/
4 https://designthinking.ideo.com/
5 For example, Rethinking Assessment's digital learner profile: the pilot is discussed in this blog: https://rethinkingassessment.com/rethinking-blogs/rethinking-assessm ent-digital-learner-profile-pilots-learnings-so-far/
6 Peter M. Senge, *The Fifth Discipline: The Art and Practice of the Learning Organisation* (Random House Business, 2006).
7 www.theguardian.com/environment/2020/jan/07/honeybees-deaths-almonds-hives-aoe
8 Koen Bartels and Nick Turnbull, 'Relational Public Administration: A synthesis and heuristic classification of relational approaches', *Public Management Review* (2019). Advance online publication. https://pure.manchester.ac.uk/ws/portalfiles/portal/ 103375510/PMR_relationalPA_Bartels_Turnbull_AAM.pdf
9 Russell Bishop, *Teaching to the North-East: Relationship-based Learning in Practice* (NZCER Press, 2019).
10 See for example, E.D. Hirsch, Jnr, *Why Knowledge Matters: Rescuing Our Children from Failed Educational Theories* (Harvard Education Press, 2016).
11 Sarah Moreland-Russell, Marissa Zwald, and Shelley D. Golden, 'Policy help needed, experience required: Preparing practitioners to effectively engage in policy', *Health Promotion Practice* 17, no. 5 (2016): 648–55.
12 Jeremy Oldfield and Steph Ainsworth, 'Decentring the "resilient teacher": Exploring interactions between individuals and their social ecologies', *Cambridge Journal of Education* 52, no. 4 (2022): 409–30. www.tandfonline.com/doi/full/10.1080/ 0305764X.2021.2011139
13 Russell Bishop, *Teaching to the North-East: Relationship-based Learning in Practice* (NZCER Press, 2019).

7 Towards a better model

There is nothing inevitable about the way education policy is made in England, as the examples from different countries show us. While it is true that the way things are currently done is a product of our history, we do not need to be constrained by the past. We need to understand why our policy-making processes are inefficient and often damaging, so that we can make things better for the future.

Some may feel this is naive, that the complexity of the system and the pressures on key players make change impossible. We disagree. There needs to be a will for a better approach to emerge, but our proposals for future policy development are not grounded on hope but on a set of principles and practices that can lead to better outcomes for everybody in the system – for politicians, think tanks, union leaders, schools, teachers, parents and, most importantly, pupils.

People have often called for new approaches.[1] It is increasingly clear that without new ways of making education policy, we are unlikely to be able to tackle the systemic issues that currently impact so negatively on pupils, teachers, leaders, and educational settings. Policy-makers and system leaders need to commit to finding a better approach, and our proposals offer some practical steps.

As the previous chapter showed, there is no shortage of ideas about how to develop policy more effectively, including through design-thinking, systems-led approaches and relational policy-making. But the complexity of the world in which we operate can mean that every policy approach leads to policy sclerosis so things just don't get done. We need to take elements of each of these approaches and combine them with a practical realism. This is about finding ways to better understand the world as it is, rather than as you want to think it is, and finding ways to improve honestly and incrementally. The imperative to make progress (through practical steps to support delivery) helps to avoid inertia.

Our proposals for better education policy-making take account of different theoretical approaches, with a focus on making progress without falling into a trap of simplistic compromise. They attempt to understand the motivations that drive different players and organisations, but within a framework that prompts each one to move beyond their own narrow interests for the wider good of the education system. Our proposals are based on three key principles and the practices that should flow from them.

DOI: 10.4324/9781032651057-8

Principles

In order to improve education policy-making in England, policy-making needs to be:

1 Collaborative – the system should be hard-wired for collaboration rather than competition, and the concept of 'co-production' needs to be reclaimed as a positive way of operating rather than seen as a sign of weak compromise;
2 Iterative – policy improvements should be gradual rather than 'big bang', allowing for appropriate risk-taking and experimentation, piloting, evaluation and improvement, and finally effective roll-out; and
3 Long term – we must get beyond the short-termism that has blighted so much education policy-making, in order to build a coherent system that avoids political whims and knee-jerk reactions.

Principle 1: Collaborative policy-making

The education system is increasingly competitive, driven by policies aimed at attaining higher league table positions, whether as individual schools or as a nation, while centralisation of policy-making sidelines the expertise and realities of teachers. Education itself though is hard-wired for collaboration: heads and teachers work together to plan and teach, building professional networks as needed to provide the best education possible. We need to redress the balance. That means starting at the top of the policy-making process, looking at those who wield the most power and designing ways in which they can operate more collaboratively.

This amounts to a decision to do two things: to pool power and to seek solutions acceptable to all. Both of these concepts have become unfashionable in recent years – in the education space and elsewhere – but both are essential to support collective improvement. Collaboration relies on a commitment to work together, to understand and be willing to subvert short-term or narrow self-interest and organisational gain for a wider benefit to the system, and to accept that progress will not be perfect.

Some models for collaboration

Models for collaboration need to be systemic rather than whimsical. Collaboration happens all the time and has been a feature of policy-making even during those times when one group (generally government) has dominated. Even people who disagree on most things, including government ministers and union general secretaries, have found ways to continue to talk and listen to one another. But collaboration is more than just being in a room together, finding slightly better ways to impose a policy idea, or listening in order to build more comprehensive arguments to oppose one.

Currently, the most common form of collaboration is stakeholder engagement. Each organisation can draw up a list of those with an interest and determine how to work with them on developing and delivering a policy. A common tool is the 'stakeholder grid' (see Figure 7.1, p. 98), which divides stakeholders up into four categories based on the level of power and interest each stakeholder is deemed to have.

Table 7.1 Some models for collaboration

Model	How it could work	Benefits	Drawbacks
Improved stakeholder engagement	Using current networks and approaches but gathering views more broadly and earlier in the process.	Easy to establish and could have an instant impact on how policy is developed.	Easy to dismantle. Easy to 'game' by parties acting in bad faith. Hard to know a full range of views is being gathered and easy for bias to operate.
Social Partnership (WAMG[2] Version 2)	A regular policy-making forum between government and unions, extending beyond schools to early years, further, and higher education.	Creates a space for transparent and confidential conversations between key organisations. Engagement can improve implementation.	Excludes most of the system still. Relies on unions faithfully representing the profession. Could suffer from competition between unions.
Co-production	Changing the policy-making approach so that all policy is co-produced by organisations and key people working together in regular meetings.	Easy to establish, brings in organisations and perspectives from across the sector. Can include individuals and experts as well as organisations.	Group selection remains open to bias. Harder to maintain confidentiality (to support challenging discussions). Less experience of policy-making amongst some group members.
Sortition	A group of education professionals is randomly selected on a regular basis to be seconded into the civil service for a fixed period and integrated into the policy-making process.	Those involved in delivering education are directly involved in making policy. Brings policy-makers closer to the profession and the profession closer to the policy-making process.	Novel and potentially expensive. Randomness can be a weakness – you do not know who you will get. It will take time for amateurs to understand how policy-making works. Teachers have little time to engage. The policy-making professionals (e.g. civil servants) could dominate.

Each quadrant will have a different level of engagement. In the bottom left, those with the least power and interest but with a broad connection to education are monitored in case they do or say anything problematic. In the bottom right, those with little power but a strong interest in a policy are kept informed, so that they understand the policy intent but are not given any role in shaping it. It is important to satisfy those in the top right, who have substantial power (especially to disrupt if they are unhappy) but little interest in the area, by offering the chance to

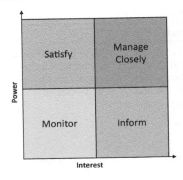

Figure 7.1 A stakeholder grid

express views and to be involved if issues arise. Finally, the 'key stakeholders', those who know a lot about a policy area, have clear and strong views, and have the power to help make a policy successful or to disrupt it, are managed closely, involved often, and given the opportunity to help shape the policy. Where they are likely to disrupt, policy-makers will need to plan mitigations to manage their opposition.

The stakeholder engagement approach is common across multiple sectors and industries, and has been part of the box of tricks for management consultants for many years. It helps those working on policy development and implementation manage the reaction of those affected and improves the chances of a policy being successful. But when we talk about individuals in current policy-making, we do not mean those affected by a policy (for example, classroom teachers), but rather key individuals who are perceived to have particular influence (for example, academics with relevant research, union officials or politicians who have been vocal on an area of policy). This means engaging with strong views rather than collective wisdom, which helps to explain why so many policies lack a clear understanding of practical implementation. It also assumes that key organisations are truly representative. But teachers may have a range of views, and the assumption that membership organisations faithfully represent all of their members is not necessarily true or possible.

Ultimately, stakeholder engagement can feel more like stakeholder management or 'handling'. Those involved in drawing up their grids of stakeholders are operating with their own biases, as of course are the stakeholders. Those whose views do not align with the policy intent are managed rather than listened to in an exercise to implement a policy already determined rather than to consider the best evidence and information. This is reinforced by the artificial movement of key stakeholders – those who already agree with a policy – into the 'manage closely' category, who are given greater access to information and decision-makers and act as an echo chamber rather than providing proper challenge.

Improved stakeholder engagement would mean building conversations with a broader range of 'interested parties' much earlier in the process, thinking carefully about how to engage with individuals as well as groups involved in or impacted by the policy. All forms of stakeholder engagement could be improved, whether by broadening working groups and commissions or improving consultation processes to go beyond asking how a policy that is already decided could be tweaked or better implemented. Because policy-makers are often far removed from the day-to-day business of schools and classrooms, conversations between civil servants and teachers, parents, children, and young people would give opportunities for the realities of school life to be better understood. It could also give those on the ground, who are impacted by policy, the opportunity to understand some of the constraints of policy-making.

Social partnership, as described in Chapter 4, creates a regular forum for engagement between the government and teaching unions on both development and delivery of policy. It has the significant advantage that policy can be discussed in private so that all parties can afford to be more open with one another. While in the past social partnership focused on schools policy primarily, separate and coordinated groups could be established to cover other areas of education policy – further and higher education, the skills sector, early years, or SEND, for example. It would also need to broaden the range of unions involved.

The importance of a space to discuss policy in a confidential way should not be under-estimated. As we set out in Chapter 2, even those at the top of organisations are trapped by the dynamics operating within the organisations they lead. They are bound to reflect the prevailing beliefs of their organisations, which makes compromise difficult. A confidential space enables those involved to entertain contrary ideas and to engage more openly. It also allows decisions to emerge that are shaped to respond to specific concerns, so that everybody involved can claim they made a positive difference to the outcome.

There are nonetheless drawbacks that need careful mitigation. First, social partnership places huge influence in the hands of the education unions and excludes other organisations with expert views and representative memberships (how would the Chartered College of Teaching – with more members than, say, the Association of School and College Leaders – be involved?). More challenging is the competition between education unions, which can mean policy discussions are viewed through the lens of inter-union competition as much as improving educational outcomes. And then there are the different motivations of all partners, which can lead to conversations about one policy coloured by an intent to support or undermine broader aims.

Wider co-production of policy could both expand the pool of those involved in discussions and broaden the policy areas to be discussed. It could bring together representative organisations, key experts and academics, and think tanks around a broad policy area – say further education – rather than a single issue (such as the Expert Advisory Group on Maths to 18).[3] Co-production groups would have a degree of permanence, could have the same principles of confidentiality and openness as social partnership, and would be better able to look across different policy initiatives and make connections. Successful co-production relies on a well-organised process so that information can be shared in a timely way and evidence can be considered properly by all involved. This has historically placed a premium on the importance of the civil servants administering this process, meaning that everyone must have faith in the impartiality and engagement of the civil service – something that will take time to re-establish in the current low-trust environment.

Co-production approaches remain subject to the biases that exist in the system in the selection of membership and the issues that are considered. It is also inevitable that the more people involved, the harder it is to maintain confidentiality, especially where members have a particular agenda to pursue and might see the leaking of information to be advantageous to that agenda in the short term. Involving a broader pool in co-production means there are more people helping to decide issues who have less experience of the complexities and necessary trade-offs involved in policy-making and delivery. This can be mitigated somewhat by establishing long-term structures to help everybody involved to understand the benefits of longer-term engagement rather than seeking short-term gain, but where there are more people involved it will always be harder to keep them working together.

The most radical approach here is sortition, based on the operation of ancient Athenian democracy in which eligible citizens were selected by lot to form the government of the city. This model is still used today, most notably in the selection of juries for the court system but also in a variety of local and national citizens' assemblies, as described in Chapter 5. It could be adapted to select a group of education professionals to provide input into policy-making and delivery. Such an approach would bring those involved in implementing policy directly into the decision-making process and avoid the need for assumptions to be made by representative organisations. The randomness of sortition would also increase the likelihood that those selected would offer a fairer reflection of the different views of the profession. Another benefit would be to increase professionals' understanding of the complexities and trade-offs involved in policy-making, which should make it harder for bad policy to emerge in the future and easier for longer-term thinking to gain traction. Figure 7.2 shows a suggested approach to sortition.

It would of course be expensive and complex to organise the selection of participants, to work with their schools and settings to arrange for them to spend time in government, to support them to understand their role, and ensure they are able to properly engage in discussions. Teachers and school leaders have a prohibitive workload, and there are too few of them in the system already. Who is eligible would need careful thought as would how participants are organised (by sector, e.g. early years, schools, FE, HE? By specialism, e.g. subject, phase? By

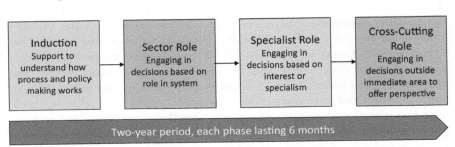

Figure 7.2 A proposed sortition approach and cycle

interest?) and there are questions about how parental and youth voices should be considered. There is a risk too that civil servants could dominate the process. Considerable efforts would also need to be made to ensure that participants understand how policy-making works so that they are able to contribute effectively, in particular considering the interconnectedness of decisions.

In all of these models of collaboration, we must not lose sight of the fact that – in the final analysis – ministers are the ones making decisions. That is an important principle of our current system of representative democracy and not one that should be lightly undermined. Collaboration will not mean that ministers must agree with ideas, recommendations, or decisions made by a group, however representative. But ministerial decisions would be considerably better informed by a collaborative process, which would help to provide greater clarity on the implications of different policy and delivery options. Ministers may feel constrained by this, but they will have a better understanding of the likely challenges to their ideas. They could still choose to pursue a policy that runs contrary to the thinking of a collaborative process but would have a better understanding of the issues and the likelihood of failure.

Perhaps the biggest challenge is that of ego. Few people in positions of power attain those lofty heights without a strong sense of who they are and their own ability to navigate the world in the best way. That is as true of union general secretaries as it is of politicians, of leaders of sector organisations as headteachers, of civil servants as academics. A belief in one's own abilities and judgement is not a bad thing. What is problematic is when that belief takes you beyond the bounds of your own knowledge and experience. It is hard to say 'I don't know', particularly when the stakes are high but, as we have established in Chapters 1–3, so many involved in shaping education policy simply do not know what they are talking about. How could they? The system is vast, the interactions complex, the consequences hard to be certain of. Yet they are all under pressure to give instant views on subjects about which they cannot help but be largely ignorant. Collaboration should be seen as a way of improving policy-making and implementation, and of giving all key people involved a greater level of understanding and protection when making necessary but difficult decisions.

Principle 2: Iterative policy-making

Given the complexities of the education landscape, it would be astonishing for any policy intervention to be perfect immediately (or, indeed, ever). Most people would accept the need for ideas to be tested and improved, to learn from delivery challenges, to evaluate the impact of any actions, and consider the outcomes against the intention. But actually, very little of this happens in the policy-making space, at least not overtly and not in a structured way. Inevitably, this leads to a lack of learning, a tendency to get defensive and to refuse to consider downsides, and for too many policy ideas to be dropped too early because they are not achieving their often-unrealistic aims. Perhaps the worst are those policy ideas that seem to come up again and again, repeating bad ideas rather than iterating to develop better options. As Einstein probably didn't say:[4] 'Insanity is doing the same thing over and over again, and expecting different results.' And we could add, 'Complete madness is doing it because you didn't even know it had been tried already.'

The importance of iteration is the opportunity to try things out, to make changes – hopefully improvements – and to learn from ideas that 'work' and those that don't.

Some models for iteration

Within the policy cycle, there are a number of moments where evaluations can be carried out, lessons learned, and changes made.

Table 7.2 Some models for iteration

Model	How it could work	Benefits	Drawbacks
End (or fixed) point evaluation	Similar to now, but with a commitment to build in evaluation as the policy is developed and systems to ensure policy learning is captured and shared.	Easy to build from the current model. Allows for policy to be implemented at scale and evaluated over time. Builds in policy learning as part of the process.	Can feel like money wasted if policy is unsuccessful or ended anyway. Lessons are easy to ignore as people move on or the political landscape changes.
Prototyping	Early in the policy process; as ideas are being generated, many models are built and tested.	Happens before much cost is incurred and before people become invested in a particular solution. Can engage more people in policy thinking.	Involves (large) investment of time at the beginning of the process. Difficult if ministers have already decided the solution. Does not provide statistically valid data
Better piloting	Using current approaches and a broader range of settings at earlier stages. The goal may be to decide whether to carry on developing this approach or whether to roll it out more widely.	Allows testing of the practicalities of implementation and to check if the policy is likely to achieve what was intended. Can highlight interactions between the new policy and other parts of the system. Engages professionals.	Is expensive and public so there may be little room for change. Those involved can feel under pressure to make the policy work rather than learning.
Ongoing review	Built in as policy is developed. Review of a broad area (e.g. curriculum) rather than a single initiative, with a planned programme of revision over a long period of time.	Important for long-term outcomes. Clear how and when things might change. More likely to see and understand system effects and interactions. Changes made over time rather than 'stop–start'.	Requires a long-term view of policy-making. Small changes made over time may change the direction and outcomes of policy without democratic oversight.

As with collaboration, it is important that iterative policy-making is systemic to build real policy learning, rather than bolt-on evaluations that nobody stays around to review. Various forms of evaluation happen in our current system, some of them with genuine potential for policy to change or even be dropped altogether. But the motivation to evaluate and learn is low when changes can take years to impact, can have effects in places we might not expect, and when responsibility for policy and its impacts can be lost in ministerial reshuffles or changes in government. It is often difficult to tell how much of an impact a specific policy has and what other factors might be in play.

For iterative policy-making to work, we need to be clear about what needs to be tested, which means involving analysts and researchers at early stages in the process. We need a realistic policy timetable, with sufficient time for a policy to be implemented before making decisions about whether to continue. We need evaluation built into the policy-making cycle, with a commitment to learn from them before new policy is developed, as well as processes to ensure lessons will be shared across policy areas and over time. And we need systems of review for those many aspects of policy that we know will need to change over time, such as curriculum or teacher development, so that changes can be properly planned for and evaluations can build a comprehensive picture.

It is important to have end or fixed-point evaluations of policy. While few policies are intended to be short term, many will have points where decisions need to be made about how or whether to continue, while others have a fixed pot of money available to them. At the end of the specified timeframe, it is important to know whether the policy has had the required effect. Politicians want to be able to show that a policy that they have championed is a success, Treasury will demand evidence that it gives value for money, and an evaluation may be needed to decide what needs to happen once this particular phase comes to an end. These require a clear understanding of the objective and the success criteria of policy to be developed, along with a strong evaluation brief, at the beginning of the process.

One major drawback of this kind of iterative policy-making is that a great deal of money and time is spent before any lessons are learnt. Where a policy is not successful, it can be more comfortable for policy-makers to move swiftly on than to carry out a full evaluation. Lessons are lost because they do not seem relevant for new situations or simply because there is no-one who is tasked with reflecting on the old policy. When a 'new' policy is devised, even a few years later, there may be no institutional memory of previous similar policy, let alone its evaluation.

So, for end or fixed-point evaluations to better lead to iterative policy-making, both targets and evaluations must be developed alongside the policy itself. There must also be systems in place for storing lessons learned, in ways that are accessible for new policies and not just in long reports that might seem relevant only to the policy that has been evaluated.

The idea of prototyping comes directly from design thinking. Early and quick testing means that many more innovative ideas can be considered, with little risk or cost. These could be at a 'story-board' stage, where those who would implement the policy try out in an imaginative form what it might be like. Later in the development process, it could involve slightly more developed models trialled in a single school, or across a MAT or a local authority. These are not designed to be representative but are an opportunity to try a small part of a larger idea, or to try some different ideas in different places. The intention is to decide which ideas are worth pursuing further, but also to engage with professionals and pupils to find new ideas. This kind of work is already done by organisations outside government, in some independent schools, and in research projects led by schools and universities, for example.

Prototyping is difficult where a policy has already been announced and ministers are wedded to a particular approach. This is a particular danger when manifestos are being developed, and as Green and White Papers expand on those manifesto commitments. There is very little chance that when Michael Gove proposed changes to the exam system,[5] which were billed as a return to O levels,[6] there could have been any kind of prototyping. But a party that commits to reviewing the qualifications system could open the door to a range of different organisations and schools developing ideas, offering opportunities for policy-makers to learn lessons before making firm commitments.

All major policies should be piloted, and this is an evaluation process that happens already. It often takes place at a point where the decision has been made to go ahead and is used to iron out implementation issues. Those who are opposed to, or unsure of, a policy are invited to observe, in order to try to bring them on board – the unions were invited to observe pilot phonics checks, for example, although this did not make them any less opposed to the policy. A pilot can form part of the communications plan for a policy, with those who carry them out giving supportive quotes. As piloting is carried out at a later stage, people have already decided for or against the policy. At this stage, it is costly to find that an intervention does not work, both in terms of real cost and in reputation, so evaluation is more likely to look for evidence of whether it is being faithfully implemented or to understand what support will be needed in order to make the policy successful. It misses an opportunity to look at whether the policy is meeting its objectives and how it interacts with other parts of the system. It can be made easier to implement, but that is not the same as building better policy.

Occasionally, pilots include a small number of different ideas implemented at the same time. For example, in 2014, three different models of baseline assessment were piloted. This is different from prototyping, as it is later in the process and interventions are more complete. Sometimes unions and others are invited to be part of the steering group for pilots and other evaluations, shaping the criteria and the process. Having more open information about the process can enable other organisations to carry out evaluations at the same time.[7]

Ongoing review is perhaps the hardest to build into the system. It is less about proving the success (or otherwise) of a policy and more about accepting that policies need to change as other parts of the system change. It recognises that policy-making does not end with publishing a policy document; implementation is part of the policy-making process and policies change when they hit the ground and as they become familiar, and so this approach involves planning for ongoing review of implementation: are teachers changing what they do over time as different evidence becomes available? While evaluations are often limited to using outcomes data to monitor success – a rise in phonics check scores is used to indicate the success of the phonics policy, for example – ongoing review would consider a wider range of measures – perhaps the impact of phonics teaching on enjoyment of reading – or a longer-term measure such as GCSE English passes. It would plan for continued review of the research. Ongoing review can also be used to identify trends and changes, to note how policies interact, and to make changes to ensure a policy still works – or changes – when something new happens.

For iterative policy-making to be successful in building effective policies, there needs to be a clear understanding of the evidence that will be sought. At different times in the process, different types of evidence may be more helpful than others, but it is easy to become fixated on a single method of evaluation. Right now, the focus on 'what works' leads to a reliance on meta-analyses, while the importance of standardisation leads us to global league tables. Teacher- and academic research are sidelined or a single academic (think E.D Hirsch on a knowledge-based curriculum[8]) or research study (such as Clackmannanshire for synthetic phonics[9]) is highlighted above all others. Different forms of evidence have their benefits, but each also has limitations and iterative policy-making must take those into account. It also requires an honest approach to the evidence, attempting to understand the problems that are identified and not cherry-picking the results that tell the story you want to tell.

One of the dangers of iterative policy-making is that small changes over time can lead a policy in a different direction than originally envisaged or promised. Evaluation over time needs to remain true to the original objectives or to be transparent where those objectives change. Evaluation reports will come in long after the original architects of a policy have moved on, and there will need to be systems in place to remind those involved to receive and reflect on the outcomes.

Iterative policy-making should require testing in 'extreme circumstances' or special situations. This could be different types of schools, children with different needs and characteristics, teachers at different career stages or of different subjects etc. Too often, a policy is rolled out having been shown to work in most circumstances that then turns out to be impossible to implement in certain places. The 2019 Ofsted Education Inspection Framework (EIF)[10] turned out to add immensely to workload in primary schools where teachers may have a number of subject specialisms, and to be almost unworkable in small schools with mixed age and stage classes led by two or three teachers. Testing in 'extreme circumstances' can help to see where mitigations might be needed before a policy is rolled out. At early stages, this kind of testing could also identify new ideas that could be more extensively trialled. Of course, this can be more expensive and time-consuming, but it could mean the difference between successful policy implementation and political U-turns.

The beauty of iterative policy-making is that it allows for continuous improvement in the system rather than big-bang solutions. This can be difficult in a system where politicians and political parties, as well as leaders of other organisations, differentiate themselves by developing the idea that will solve the problems. But it is vital if we are to move towards policy-making that is long term.

Principle 3: Long-term policy-making

Education is far from unique in suffering from short-termism in policy-making and many of the factors that blight other sectors are challenges for education too. It is worth stating the obvious point that education requires long-term thinking because it is at a minimum focusing on the more than a decade period of compulsory schooling (5–18), and in a broader sense covers learning from cradle to grave. These are connected periods of development and learning and benefit from a cohesive approach, but that can mean that benefits for a particular intervention may be years in the realisation and evaluating impact can be a very confused process.

Some models for long-term policy-making

Table 7.3 Some models for long-term policy-making

Model	How it could work	Benefits	Drawbacks
Build on the past	Improved systems for storing and recalling evidence from past policy interventions. A focus on continuous improvement rather than 'burning platform'.	Removes the incentive for major change on political timelines. Moves away from the narrative that everything that went before was wrong.	Less opportunity for dramatic change. Potentially less innovation. Politicians, and others, unable to develop policies that set them apart.
10-year planning	Collaborating to draw up an agreed 'whole education' plan, with short-, medium-, and long-term goals, and a system for monitoring and flexing as needed.	Gives more certainty, which builds trust. Allows time for policies to bed in and has flexibility to change in an agreed way. Built in evaluation.	Needs cross-party and cross-organisation commitment and collaboration. Takes time to develop and resources to maintain.
Futures thinking	Systematic, led by Parliament, looking at different forces that shape society, employment, and education. Developing policies focused on desired change.	Continuity. Opportunities for cross-party agreement and clarity on values. Engages people in broad discussion. Allows for innovation and future-proofing.	Complex to establish. Easy to be divorced from the realities and needs of the present. Can become a talking shop.
Systems thinking	Bring experts together within education and across different related policy areas to map systems and relationships. Work through possible short- and long-term effects and interactions of policies.	Moves away from 'unintended consequences' to make transparent decisions about conflicts and preferred options. Makes clearer the trade-offs that are needed.	Complex – can never see all the systems at play or all the possible effects. Could lead to decision paralysis as more options need to be considered.

The plague of short-termist thinking and implementation is common across governments. The political lives of ministers making key decisions are generally short and, even when there is longevity, there is little security. Creating consistency and long-term thinking across such a backdrop is extremely difficult, and the political exigencies of the day drive decision-making far more than any clear-sighted plan for the long term. It is not just politicians looking for short-term wins at the expense of long-term planning. The financial planning cycles that dominate government do not lend themselves to thinking beyond three to five-year cycles even when the electoral waters are calm, and with the political turbulence of recent years financial planning has often not been possible beyond a year, sometimes not beyond a few months.

Long-term policy-making is a natural consequence of the other changes suggested in this chapter. Collaborative and iterative policy-making approaches both benefit from and encourage longer-term thinking as they work against opportunism and quick but shallow returns on investment. Good examples of joined-up futures thinking, including from Wales, show the possibilities that are available when organisations are committed to similar goals into the long-term future. Policy that is to properly consider consequences across different parts of the system is likely to need a long-term perspective. The models outlined here are likely to overlap.

Long-term thinking must involve the past as well as the future, and so we need systems of evaluation and collation that allow policy-makers to understand what has gone before. This is an extension of iterative policy-making, involving a view across a range of policies and a broader understanding of the history and context of education policies. The drive to improve teacher professionalism since the 1970s has seen teaching become a graduate profession, the introduction of formal staff development days, and increased calls for investment, realised in policy decisions, progression, and training. Policies have built on past success up to a point, although 'political whims' have still flourished at times. Looking to the past would need to be a systematic part of policy-making that ensures policy-makers have due regard to previous interventions. It would require a commitment to long-term evaluation of the system to understand the effects of policy as contexts change and as new policies are introduced. It would, and should, constrain the instincts of politicians to rubbish the ideas of their predecessors and opponents, to suggest that education has gone wrong in some way, in order to invent exciting new ways of solving the problems.

Developing 10- (or 15-) year planning has been proposed recently by a number of prominent organisations.[11] This is different from our current model of 10-year planning, where the government of the day sets out its plan, which is roundly criticised by the opposition and other organisations, and then consults on actions within the plan rather than the plan itself. For it to be successful, it needs to be drawn up collaboratively, with an agreed vision of the future, or with an agreed mission or focus – well-rounded education or disadvantaged pupils, for example – and with goals to be reached over the period that go beyond pupil attainment. The mission should be large enough that all parts of the system need to be focused towards it – this is not a 10-year plan for school buildings or for teacher recruitment, although each of those will be essential to its success. It should allow for a considered review, based on the mission or vision, rather than sudden changes of focus or constant additions because of political or popular pressure. It would be a 'rolling' plan, with agreed points at which it could be extended or refreshed, that preferably did not coincide with general elections. A broad plan would encourage ongoing review across the system as a whole as well as over time.

The obvious drawback of this is the commitment – time, resources, political capital – needed up-front to develop the plan, along with the continuing resourcing of monitoring progress. Agreeing a plan would be difficult as values and beliefs about education are unlikely to align across political and educational divides, but a 10-year plan relies on collaboration and a willingness to find solutions that are acceptable to all.

Futures thinking (as explored in Chapter 5) is different from 10-year planning, although it needs to lead to firm plans to avoid being merely a talking shop. Policy-makers consider current trends and issues – climate change, digitalisation and AI, migration, jobs, poverty – and describe possible futures where those trends have continued. The purpose is to open up conversations about major future problems and opportunities and to consider ways of addressing them. While in some cases, scenario planning cuts across the whole government agenda, it is also possible to look more specifically at education. It could still consider similar current trends but focus on their impact on education, or it could look at more specific education trends and provide a number of 'stories' of how education might look. It is important to stress that these are not predictions of possible futures, but ways of opening up the discussion to allow for innovative ideas to be considered and for consideration of the impacts of different actions across the system. Because these scenarios are far into the future, no single political party or organisation can claim credit (or apportion blame) for the developments, opening up the possibility of identifying policy interventions that all might agree with.

Those countries and organisations that have been scenario planning in this way over a number of years have structures in place to make it work. Finland's systematic approach (see Chapter 5) is cross-parliamentary and across the whole of government activity, and has evolved over a long period of time. But it is possible to choose to use scenarios already developed and to consider their relevance in our own context. Drawbacks include the time it takes to do well, even when using pre-existing scenarios, in order to come to agreement on the issues to consider and the plausibility of particular scenarios. Developing plans from those scenarios also takes time, and each stage requires training if it is to be carried out rigorously.

Working system-wide involves the recognition that education is more than the sum of its (many) parts, and that the relationships between the parts, and between the people involved, are also key components of the system. To put it simplistically, currently we seem to make policy by focusing on a particular aspect (assessment, teacher development) and then, when we've 'solved' it, looking around at other issues that might need to change to accommodate our solution. Impacts elsewhere become 'unintended consequences' that we scramble to address.

Systems thinking requires us to understand the 'ecosystem' of education and to think systematically about the ways in which policy interventions might affect other areas, immediately and over time. It allows us to anticipate possible consequences and be honest about the trade-offs that need to be made. But working system-wide is about more than a change of mindset; there needs to be a commitment to develop system- and relationship-mapping, to map different types of feedback loops and the causes and effects of change, and to work with a range of tools to support systems thinking.[12]

Systems thinking is complex and never complete because systems are overlapping and interrelated and it is impossible to anticipate every relationship and every effect. It requires both long-term thinking and the involvement of a broad range of people and organisations for it to be effective. Everything will have consequences beyond the positive impacts that a policy seeks to have, which can make decision-making even more difficult and lead to inaction (which also has consequences). It also requires its own systems in place to ensure that it is carried out, and that the knowledge and understanding is shared so that thinking does not need to be redone from scratch every time.

Building towards a better model

Many of these models, for collaboration, iteration, and long-term thinking, require a change in behaviour from civil servants and ministers, as those who are in control of the policy-making process. But they are models that are already used by some organisations involved in policy-making, and could be more frequently and more widely used within the system.

His Majesty's Treasury (HMT) clearly has a key role to play in promoting more long-term thinking and action, and the benefits of proposals here reach beyond education. By providing a greater certainty of the proportion of national income that would be invested in education, and allowing funding to be rolled over between financial years for example, there would be more incentive to plan projects over a number of years. This would require comparable commitment from the Department for Education to operate differently, using the benefits of more collaborative and iterative policy-making to secure better decision-making and implementation.

These principles would also be supported by a stronger approach to the use of evaluation and evidence in policy-making, for example with the creation of an education equivalent of the Office for Budgetary Responsibility (OBR), with the responsibility to provide independent and verifiable evidence on the impact of policy interventions. This would need to be independent of, but funded by, government and could offer a trusted and clear-headed assessment of the promises being made by policy proposals and the impact they achieve over time.

Some people go further and seek the wider de-politicisation of education policy-making, but we judge that this is neither tenable nor desirable. What happens in the classroom, the daily lived experience of our children, must always be subject to democratic accountability. It is true that this is a weak and overplayed link by some – how many voters made their decisions in the polling booth based on the education views of each party, let alone the commitments in a manifesto or even more the unknown beliefs of ministers yet to come over whom voters have no control? But the fact that there is the potential for democratic accountability provides a necessary check to bureaucratic overreach. Moreover, we cannot conceive of a balanced, independent, and depoliticised function that would work in practice.

Instead, it is better that the power in the system – ultimately that of ministers to make final decisions in many cases (subject to their obligations to Parliament) – is recognised and constrained by more effective systems for policy-making as set out in this chapter.

Chapter summary

- A new way of policy-making should be built on three principles: collaboration, iteration, and long-term thinking.
- Models for collaboration include improved stakeholder engagement, social partnership, co-production, and sortition.
- Iterative policy-making models include fixed-point evaluation, prototyping, improved piloting, and ongoing review.
- Ideas for long-term policy-making include building on the past, 10-year planning, futures thinking, and systems thinking.
- Building these principles would involve changes in practices for all those involved in policy-making.

Notes

1 Recent examples in 2023 include the Times Education Commission and the Foundation for Education Development (FED).
2 See Chapter 5.
3 https://assets.publishing.service.gov.uk/government/uploads/system/uploads/attachment_data/file/1150741/Expert_advisory_group_on_maths_to_18_terms_of_reference.pdf
4 For example: www.history.com/news/here-are-6-things-albert-einstein-never-said
5 https://hansard.parliament.uk/Commons/2012-09-17/debates/1209177000001/ExamReform
6 www.theguardian.com/politics/2012/sep/16/michael-gove-gcses-o-levels-reform
7 Alice Bradbury and Guy Roberts-Holmes, "*They are Children...Not Robots, Not Machines*": *The Introduction of Reception Baseline Assessment* (ATL, NUT, UCL, 2016), https://discovery.ucl.ac.uk/id/eprint/1476041/1/baseline-assessment–final-10404.pdf
8 E.D. Hirsch, *Why Knowledge Matters: Rescuing Our Children from Failed Educational Theories* (Harvard University Press, 2016) and see www.coreknowledge.org/our-approach/knowledge-based-schools/case-content-rich-curriculum/
9 Rhona Johnston and Joyce Watson, *The Effects of Synthetic Phonics Teaching on Reading and Spelling Attainment: A Seven Year Longitudinal Study* (Scottish Executive, 2005), https://dera.ioe.ac.uk/id/eprint/14793/1/0023582.pdf
10 Ofsted, *Education Inspection Framework: Overview of Research* (2019), https://assets.publishing.service.gov.uk/media/6034be17d3bf7f265dbbe2ef/Research_for_EIF_framework_updated_references_22_Feb_2021.pdf
11 Times Education Commission and the Foundation for Education Development (FED).
12 The systems-thinking toolkit for civil servants sets out a range of tools, www.gov.uk/government/publications/systems-thinking-for-civil-servants/toolkit

8   Better Policy-Making Toolkit

In the previous chapter, we set out three key principles that should underpin education policy-making: collaboration, iteration, and long-term thinking. Framing policy-making in these ways would have a powerful, and positive impact on the development and implementation of education policy, but it is complex to achieve because it involves multiple players making the choice to engage. In particular, those with power to make decisions and those with influence over implementation need to be involved, otherwise any change will be cosmetic rather than substantive. We hope that the processes we have explored add to the ongoing pressure for change in our policy-making systems. In the meantime, this chapter builds a toolkit to improve policy-making now while working towards systemic change. Whether you are leading a policy-making process, involved in implementing policy, or advocating for change, the toolkit in this chapter is intended to help.

The toolkit (see Figure 8.1) consists of four stages to work through as policy is being designed, with each stage repeating three consistent elements. The four stages are points of decision – what is it you need to determine at this point? The three elements consider the process – how should you go about determining it? Of course, as with all policy processes, none of the stages or elements are clearcut and it is likely that they will blend into each other. Nor is this a linear process, and each stage may be revisited many times.

Mindset

Before we get into the detail of the toolkit, it is important to make sure that we are operating with the right mindset. This toolkit is not a checklist but a process that needs to be engaged with properly. That means making a commitment to working and thinking in particular ways: building relationships; being open to learning; and focusing on children and young people above all else. These set the culture within which policy-making takes place, and are intended to apply to all who are involved. They should underpin the development of processes and the ways in which people work together.

DOI: 10.4324/9781032651057-9

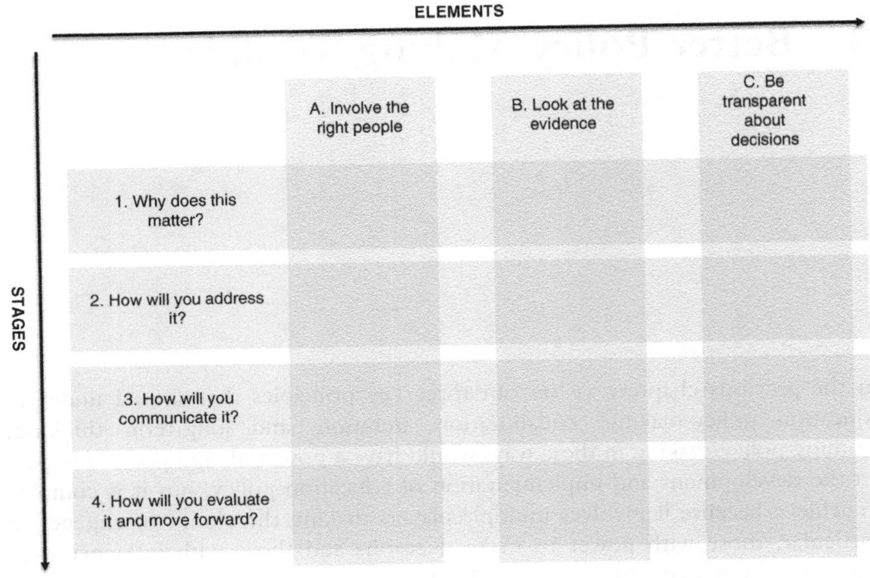

ELEMENTS

	A. Involve the right people	B. Look at the evidence	C. Be transparent about decisions
1. Why does this matter?			
2. How will you address it?			
3. How will you communicate it?			
4. How will you evaluate it and move forward?			

STAGES

Figure 8.1 The Better Policy-Making Toolkit – partial version

Building relationships

We have already set out in Chapter 7 why involving a diverse range of people and views is important for successful policy-making. The commitment to building relationships goes further, setting out the expectation that every encounter has as a focus the strengthening of relationships. These may be between policy-makers and schools or between government and unions, for example. But policy development and implementation also offer opportunities to strengthen relationships within these groups, with policy-makers actively creating opportunities for professionals, parents, and others to work together to build a better education system.

Partnership working often underpins education, with subject specialists or teachers in particular phases coming together to plan, to evaluate, and to learn with each other. This could be extended to involve conversations about policy issues with groups from different areas – many organisations and unions already build opportunities for this. Alternatively, it may be that mixing groups of parents, teachers, and employers in local areas would lead to fruitful conversations about ways in which these people could work together on other issues of importance.

There are many points of disagreement between those involved in education, and this commitment is not about getting everyone to agree. Building relationships requires an openness to listen, and a willingness to understand, to recognise that the way in which we see the world is not the only way. At its most simple, a commitment to relationship means refusing to pigeonhole people, even for clever soundbites, and moving away from the dichotomous labels – 'trad' vs 'prog' – often used to demonise the 'opposite' camp. For any long-term planning to survive changes in government it is vital that those involved are committed to building open and honest relationships with people who have very different views, experiences, and values.

Learning

A policy-making model with a commitment to relationships leads quickly into one that requires genuine learning. It could be argued that we have moved a long way in this direction with the commitment to evidence-based or evidence-informed policy, randomised controlled trials, and dedication to data. But too often, the evidence is used to support our arguments rather than to challenge our thinking. It is used to demonstrate a pressing need for change rather than to understand the system as it is.

Policy-making with a commitment to learning means genuinely trying to understand the arguments of opponents, not in order to demolish those arguments but to find common ground on which to build. It means considering the evidence from those whose positions you might disagree with, or from places you believe are biased, for example, politically aligned think tanks, unions, or universities, not in order to dismiss it ('they would say that, wouldn't they') but to build a bigger picture of the issue.

Of course, decisions have to be taken, and a commitment to learning is not about having to compromise nor about making sure everyone agrees with the decision. It is about recognising that education is complex, and there are aspects of it that you might not have considered. It means openness to the idea that you might be wrong or that there are different ways of looking at a problem. People will always have strong views, particularly about education, and our model seeks to encourage that. But a commitment to learning means not allowing those views to close down conversations. Building a commitment to learning would mean giving sufficient time in these conversations to listen to each other's experiences and for policy-makers to engage with open minds and not closed questions.

Children and young people

As we have said before, it is easy to suggest that everyone involved in education is working towards the same aims – a better future for children and young people. But a commitment to children and young people must mean more than that bland statement. This is not a wishy-washy belief in the importance of children for our future, but one that requires hard-nosed analysis of the impact of policies on children and young people now, as well as our intentions for the future. It means a commitment to unpicking what we mean by 'better'; to understanding how our actions influence future possibilities; and to greater transparency about the futures we are working towards. It also means thinking about the experiences those children and young people are having now. Young people are part of their communities, and schools are supporting their engagement now as well as preparing them for the future.

Too often, policy-makers are a long way removed from children and young people, or they extrapolate from their experience with their own children or those of friends. It is important that those in power listen to the experiences of teachers, and others, with expertise in children's development and learning. But a commitment to children and young people involves engaging directly with them too. It involves understanding their contexts, their struggles and aspirations, and ensuring that policy-making is focused on making their lives better now and in the future. It involves ensuring that their needs are not a poor second to the needs of the economy or older people. And it means balancing long-term planning with a real focus on what children and young people need now rather than constantly making them 'ready for' whatever we think is coming next.

These three commitments must underpin each of the stages and elements we outline. Every stage of policy-making should lead to better relationships, deeper learning, and a clearer focus on the lives of children and young people. The way in which every process is developed, whether engaging with people, interrogating evidence, or communicating decisions, should improve relationships, learning, or the focus on children and young people, and hopefully all three. While there will always be a power imbalance – someone must make the final decisions, and someone holds the money – these commitments allow for a more genuine interaction between all those involved in making, implementing, and experiencing policy.

Stages

Stage 1: Why does this matter?

Before anything else, it is important to make sure we achieve enough clarity for the issue to be addressed. The problems that we set out to solve in education are not straightforward issues with a clear cause and solution, but rather 'wicked' problems with interdependent factors that are complex and constantly changing. Right now we could do with a reset to reach a broader consensus on the key issues, how education sits within and impacts society and the economy, and how it needs to change to meet current and future needs. We need to set out why education matters. But Stage 1 is important for clarifying more immediate issues too.

The most common mistake during this stage is jumping to a 'solution' rather than starting from the issue(s) to be addressed. As an example, the data suggest attendance at schools is getting worse, meaning more children (and more likely the most vulnerable children) are missing out on education, affecting their outcomes. Rather than being clear about what this means, too often policy-makers jump directly to a preferred answer (for example, parents on benefits will lose these if their children do not attend school).[1]

Such an approach is problematic because it presupposes a shared understanding of the fundamental issue without being clear. Is the issue one of attendance (that being in school is a virtue in itself), attainment (being in school is necessary for learning), tackling disadvantage (improving attendance is how we will close the 'attainment gap'), or sanction (families on benefits should be expected to behave in a particular way and punished when they do not)? Lack of clarity at the beginning means that, as a policy is developed and rolled out and changes happen in response to circumstances, it morphs into something unlikely to achieve the impact intended.

Lack of clarity means that ideas are not developed with sufficient rigour or alternatives properly considered. Put bluntly, how can you be sure an idea is the best one if you have not been clear about what it is trying to achieve and what the alternatives are? In the worst scenarios, alternatives are discouraged because they could confuse decision-making or reduce the commitment to an idea already decided. Everybody becomes caught up in the specifics of an idea rather than the underpinning issue – ministers because an idea can feel appealingly simple, civil servants because (almost above all things) they crave certainty from ministers, unions because they can use it to advance their own narrative, schools because they have something concrete to respond to.

Leaping to the solution ignores the complexity in the system, the connections between policy areas, and the likely unintended consequences. For example, what would the wider implications be of sanctioning parents on benefits if their children fail to attend school, quite apart from whether the idea would actually improve attendance? How would this affect policy to reduce poverty, and what other services would be affected if this pushed families further into poverty? All of these things can be considered as a policy idea is taken forward, but by waiting until after a commitment is made, time and energy is often wasted.

It is easy for those outside government also to leap to the proposed solution, building arguments about why it will not solve the problem or what other problems it will cause. Attempting to understand and influence the thinking about the fundamental issue(s) can lead to a less confrontational approach, which is essential to building better long-term policy. At the very least it will allow clearer arguments to be made and different solutions to be proposed. And as you focus on the commitments, it is important to think about how the processes you develop in Stage 1 help to build relationships that enable you to listen to what really matters.

Individuals involved in the process can work together to develop better clarity about the issue to be addressed and how it relates to possible or preferable futures, in order to support long-term and iterative policy planning. In particular, it will be helpful to identify how the issue affects children and young people, both now and in the future. This should be done as comprehensively as possible from the very start of the process. Simplicity is key, as long as it increases understanding.

Stage 1: Why does this matter?

- Ask difficult questions
- Map issues and their relationships
- Be clear how issues are being defined
- Build processes to keep issues and key questions updated

Stage 2: How will you address it?

Addressing the issues involves making decisions about both the intervention to pursue and its implementation. Being clearer at Stage 1 makes it possible to better explore solutions and show how they are addressing the issue and are possible to implement. Stage 2 requires better systems mapping that considers the impact of proposals on different parts of the system within education and across other sectors, as well as over time.

Implementation is too often the poor relation of policy-making, rarely being considered in the decision-making process. The assumption is that all the hard thinking has to go into deciding what to do – the grubby business of actually doing it is not the concern of the rarefied brains shaping the future of the nation. Many government departments still have a separation between policy formulation and implementation. This is sometimes an internal separation, other times through overt organisational structures – for example, the split between the Department for Education and the Standards and Testing Agency (STA).

Everyone working in education has probably experienced an instruction from Whitehall that is astonishing in its naivety in terms of delivery because of timescale, cost, staffing, capacity, or intent. Think tanks, unions, and academics can also come up with impractical policy solutions, although they rarely have to implement them. The person who suffers most from a poor implementation plan is usually the teacher in front of a class of children trying to make sense of rushed curriculum changes or the headteacher juggling policy directives that all need implementing at once.

Implementation is often hampered by time. There is a general view amongst policy-makers that quicker is always better: if you have the right answer you must get it delivered as quickly as possible; after all, we are talking about improving the lives of children so who would not want that to happen now? Most people involved in policy-making only have a short time to make a difference and want to push through changes to gain the credit or to embed a change which ties the hands of a political opponent. With much education policy, the time at which an intervention can make a difference does not last long – all of which can lead to knee-jerk responses.

Artificial timetables often dictate policy-making decisions. The most obvious example is the Treasury spending review cycle (in recent years, a cycle that has barely covered a year – see Chapter 3), creating deadlines for implementation *and* showing impacts that are completely divorced from the actual needs of any given issue. But without wanting to lean too heavily on *Yes, Minister* cliches, as Sir Humphrey says to his minister, Jim Hacker, 'It takes time to do things "now".'[2]

There are also times when those setting timetables are too cautious, seeking more time than is needed to get a policy delivered. At best, implementation might then happen earlier (a triumph of bureaucracy!) or at worst it takes more time (it was always a fearfully difficult implementation, which is why more time was asked for!). The next line in the *Yes, Minister* quote above belongs to Jim Hacker: 'The three articles of civil service faith: it takes longer to do things quickly; it's more expensive to do them cheaply; it's more democratic to do them in secret.'[3]

Policy and its implementation are often not well planned. Business and industry recognise that project management is key, that they need a clear plan of what needs to happen, in what sequence, to make it work; otherwise they are risking their reputation and possibly their financial viability. Governments of all colours are notoriously bad at delivering large-scale projects. The Institute for Government was very scathing of the current government's (lack of) delivery of the HS2 project, noting that 'infrastructure decision-making in this country could be changed for the better ... these can be addressed by better planning, properly incentivising projects to keep to planned schedules and ensuring relevant departments and public bodies have the skills to oversee project delivery...'.[4]

Addressing the issue then requires comprehensive planning, with possible solutions and their implementation considered together. It should develop processes which will build relationships between those who will address the issue and those who are affected, and use evidence to build learning and question thinking. It will also be important to consider how the proposed solutions will impact on young people's wider circumstances as well as this particular issue.

Stage 2: How will you address it?

- Identify possible solutions
- Map the system to consider possible impacts across policy areas and over time
- Build a plan, with time frames, and set against other activity
- Share system maps and project plans

Stage 3: How will you communicate it?

Communication is essential at each stage of the policy-making process, and the same principles apply whether this is about communicating ideas and issues or decisions and implementation plans: it is a combination of what you want to say and what others need to hear. It is also about being very clear what it is you want people to do as a result of your communication: it may be that you are looking to influence people to think differently about an issue, to understand a different perspective, or to change a decision; it could be that you want to persuade people that an intervention is worth pursuing or to make sure that a policy is implemented consistently. You may be imposing a requirement to act, offering incentives for action, or providing reasons why someone should act. Methods of communication will depend on the people who need to hear the ideas, their interests, and current level of knowledge, so it is vital to decide who those people are. It is also worth considering who those people listen to, in order to think about who else to talk to.

It seems a ridiculous thing to say, but in order to implement a policy idea successfully it is important to let people know what you intend to do and why, with plenty of time for those who will implement changes to prepare. This starts with a clear explanation of the problem and the thinking that has led to the chosen solution. Not everybody will agree with that thinking and there will be challenges. Decisions need to be made about who to inform and when, with clear explanations of the timescales, particularly if they are tight – as they were, for example, as the situation unfolded during the Covid-19 pandemic. There is no single right way to communicate and the growth in social media has created both opportunities and challenges for communications teams. It is important to spend time understanding the best route for the circumstances – and testing that decision as it is rolled out.

The communication and justification of policy decisions has become something of a lost art, as successive governments have sought to find administrative efficiencies in communications teams, and ministers have been tempted to tell the story of how they want to present the world, rather than the world as it actually is. The adversarial nature of the system can mean that others can make short-term gains by misrepresenting or confusing the solution. This is particularly true in the case of controversial issues where the most political gain can be made by criticism and bluster that does little to help those who will have to understand and implement a new policy.

Communication is too often viewed as a one-way street, with policy 'announced', often by a senior politician – perhaps even the Prime Minister. Much thought is given to the venue, often a sympathetic school or important conference, but not so often in Parliament where questions might be asked. Speeches are written which outline the successes that government policy has achieved already, or the failures of the previous administration, which build a journey towards the new idea. This communication is often light on detail, leaving that to future publications, and leaving those who will be affected feeling that this is 'just one more thing they will have to do'.

It is also viewed as one-off or limited, as if once a policy is communicated it is delivered and implemented. It appears sometimes to come as a surprise to policy-makers that their vision has been translated so differently in practice.

Communication is key for ministers and civil servants charged with 'delivering' policy successfully, but it is also important for those who are looking to influence policy as it is developed and implemented. The timing of communication is crucial; too late, and the opportunity to influence constructively is lost. Where the intention is to influence the questions to be addressed, or the understanding of the problem, then the earlier the communication, the better.

What is vital at this stage is finding ways to build and to maintain dialogue, and to use conversations to build learning, for both policy-makers and those involved and affected. In particular, it is important to build real dialogue with children and young people.

Stage 3: How will you communicate it?

- Clarify your messages
- Set out what you want people to do and what needs to change
- Consider the timing – how much to communicate and when
- Build systems to hold, update, and share this information

Stage 4: How will you evaluate it and move forward?

If we are committed to iterative policy-making, it follows that we need to have the best information available from which to iterate. This means that evaluation is built into policy-making from the very beginning, and that all involved are clear what is to be measured, by when, and how. This is another reason why the clarity set out in Stage 1 is so important – if you are not clear on the problem you are trying to address, how will you know when you have made a difference?

To be clear, evaluation is often already a fundamental part of the policy-making process, but it is misused and ignored too often.

Too many evaluations are badly framed, at best complacent in understanding what needs to be tested, and at worst deliberately framed in order to find a particular result. Analysts are an essential part of the policy-making process, but may be brought in too late to shape policy thinking or will be presented with a narrow issue to evaluate rather than a broader, and more useful, set of questions. This can be just as true for external evaluations and those carried out by unions or other organisations, with funders or evaluation partners chosen and questions framed to reflect particular values, beliefs, or expected findings.

There is often too little time given for effective evaluation before decisions about continuing funding or making changes are made. This can be challenging enough with a policy that may take three or four years to complete (for example, evaluating the implementation of the Early Career Framework), but becomes almost impossible when looking at policies that may not bear fruit for more than a decade (for example, interventions in the early years that may not reflect their full benefit until a child progresses into secondary school or even into adulthood).

And then, it is rare for evaluations to be built into the policy-making cycle, with a clear effort to actually learn from them before a policy is developed. Instead, they become an add-on, sometimes undertaken with real skill and commitment but not integrated into decision-making. For example, the Teaching and Leadership Innovation Fund (TLIF) was intended to run over three years,[5] investing in innovative programmes to support teacher professional development and providing evidence to support future investments. A later decision to create the ECF and to reform NPQs meant that the TLIF quickly became seen as a short-term project without any overt, lasting impact and the evaluation of programmes was published in 2022 without any significant attempt to draw lessons for the future.[6]

Building in evaluation from the beginning means being clear about the issue in Stage 1 and its possible solutions in Stage 2, as well as developing broad success criteria at the point of policy design. It involves considering whether there are particular points when evaluation will be helpful or necessary, as well as whether there are small-scale projects and prototypes to be developed along the way. As you map the systems in Stage 2, it will be important to consider how to interpret feedback loops and evaluate broader impacts across different areas, and to build processes to share both of those with others who are developing policies in other parts of the system.

Evaluation does make policy-making slower. It takes time and requires proper expertise. It is also likely to be frustrating, being inconclusive or contradictory. Nonetheless, if we do not try to understand whether the interventions pursued are effective, we are fumbling around in the dark. So analysts should be involved at the very beginning of the policy-making process, and throughout. Evaluation methods should also be developed with the aim of building relationships to build evidence and to learn from what is surprising. And the views of children and young people should be sought throughout, as well as broader evidence of impact on them.

Stage 4: How will you evaluate it and move forward?

- Build in evaluation at the start and identify success criteria
- Map an evaluation timeline over an appropriate period of time
- Evaluate broadly across the system to identify possible unintended consequences
- Develop systems to collate evidence, and agree processes and times to share and review information and evidence, and to make changes

---

Elements

Across each of these four stages, there are three consistent elements – things you should do – to increase the chances of creating and implementing a successful policy.

Element A: Involve the right people

As we have already set out, we firmly believe that policy development should be collaborative, which obviously means engaging the right people at the right time. It is worth saying that most people involved in policy-making are committed to involving the right people, but who those 'right' people are is up for debate.

At present, the question too often comes down to whether the people to engage are already inclined to agree with a decision or are broadly sympathetic in their outlook, which means they can be considered trustworthy. We have both put together enough working groups and expert panels – both inside and outside government – to know that the thorny choice of who should be 'in the room where it happens' gets dictated by soundness (however defined) more often than expertise. The drawbacks of such an approach are clear – expertise is restricted, at significant risk of 'group think'.[7] A dangerous and self-reinforcing loop is created in which those who want to be 'in the tent' say what they think is wanted rather than what they truly believe, sometimes excused (with some justification) by the belief that it is better to be involved than not in order to ameliorate the worst elements of a policy idea.

One way to guard against this is to build better stakeholder engagement, as described in Chapter 7, ensuring that more conversations are had with a broader range of people from the earliest stages right through the process. This includes engaging those who disagree with you, the experts of contrary views, those who represent key parts of the system, and particularly 'extreme users' – those who work in small schools or with children with SEND, for example. There are many ways of involving people, from consultations and expert groups to design labs and working groups, many of which are already used by government and others, but which can always be improved.

While education policy does involve infrastructure projects (see the NAO reports on Building Schools for the Future,[8] for example), it most frequently works with people as the end recipients of policy decisions. If the capacity and capabilities of those people who will implement policy (for example, teachers) and those who will be affected by it (pupils or parents) are not properly considered, the 'delivery' of any policy will be at risk. Yet this is seldom the way that most policy is considered in England. Children and young people are rarely consulted in any meaningful way on issues that truly matter, even though they will have particular experience and views, making it extremely important to develop processes that can better involve them both in the thinking and the design of policy.

By involving people as you identify the issues and why they matter, you will come up with more ideas and potential solutions. By continuing to engage it is possible to test ideas, or at least to talk them through, before decisions are made and while policies and implementation plans are being designed. Those people will be key to your communications strategy: the best proponents of an intervention are those who have been part of designing it, as long as they are representative of the wider profession – it will be hard for a secondary headteacher to sound credible to a reception class teacher, or vice versa, because their contexts are so different, but involving both in the process allows for them both to speak to their own networks. They will be part of your evaluation cycle, and it will be helpful to circle back to those who are already involved in the policy-making process to consider the ideas that were discussed and the values and concerns that have underpinned those conversations.

However, as a policy-making process unfolds, you should also be open to speaking to different people rather than making the mistake of only engaging the same people at each stage. Even if you have tried to be open and allow challenge at the beginning of a process, those involved can become as tied to an outcome as you are and be as unwilling to accept criticism or challenge.

While this may look like we are talking specifically about those who are 'delivering' policy, it is also important for those who are offering ideas and solutions from outside government to engage in these processes. In fact, think tanks and charities are often engaged in these practices already and by engaging with them, policy-makers could mitigate some of the risks of carrying it out themselves.

Processes for involving people should form part of long-term planning. It could include planning different types of conversations over a number of years and policy issues or going back to the same groups at different times to deepen the learning and the relationships. It should also support dialogue between and learning from those with different views and expertise.

Table 8.1 Involve the right people

Element A: Involve the right people	
Stage 1: Why does this matter?	**Who does this matter to?** • Identify the people • Map their interests and concern • Involve 'extreme users' • Find the best ways to involve people
Stage 2: How will you address it?	**Who will be part of addressing it?** • Identify those who are affected – across education and beyond • Identify those who will implement • Involve them – or organisations who involve them – in prototyping and early testing
Stage 3: How will you communicate it?	**Who needs to know: what, when and how?** • Identify those who have already been involved – and those who haven't • Identify those who agree, disagree, or are indifferent • Map stakeholders: the decision-makers and the influencers • Identify those who will be affected, who are interested in, and who will implement the policy
Stage 4: How will you evaluate it and move forward?	**Who can tell you what's worked and what hasn't?** • Identify those who have been involved and/or affected, those who have benefitted and those who have not • Identify those with strong views – for and against • Map when and how you will collect views and experiences

Element B: Look at the evidence

A key indicator that you are about to make a massive mistake is that the evidence you are considering points to a single conclusion, especially if that conclusion happens to align with your own biases. Given the complexity of the world we are operating in and the myriad issues and interdependencies within the education system, evidence will always be patchy, contradictory, and confusing. Seemingly obvious solutions are not necessarily wrong, but they are not necessarily right either.

You should focus on gathering and understanding as much evidence as possible on a particular issue, using a broad approach that is open to new ideas, including those from outside education, and be prepared to be honest about where the evidence is lacking. Such an approach is, of course, supported by engaging a wide range of people as it gives them a chance to share new thoughts and ideas with you and steer you towards evidence that you might not have otherwise considered. It is important to ensure that you are also honest about the limits of your own understanding and engage specialists where that is needed – for example, analysts to help with data crunching or academics with new research.

It is always worth considering whether an issue has been considered elsewhere in the world, in the past, or in different contexts or parts of the system. This is not to suggest that there are ready-made answers, policies that we can pick off the shelf or repackage. Understanding how an issue has been addressed elsewhere should offer insights into the benefits and risks of particular solutions, as well as ideas to test in our own circumstances.

We should also think about the range of evidence that will be useful as we develop policy. Focusing on a single study, or studies with similar methodology or assumptions, may reinforce our own biases, while evidence from 'what works' should invite us to ask what we mean by 'works'. Surveys and consultations can be unrepresentative because respondents self-select – usually those who have strong opinions on an issue – or because questions are framed too narrowly. Teacher-research will be useful in some circumstances but is rarely large-scale, and prototyping or mini-trialling may not provide statistically valid data. Evidence from conversations needs to be captured, and we have seen instances where teachers have been videoed talking about the difficulties of workload and the impact on their wellbeing, which have had much greater impact on policy-makers than any data on working hours ever can.

While it is best to have a full set of evidence and information available before any decisions are made, that is likely to be impracticable both because time pressures will demand action is taken and because new evidence will emerge as a policy unfolds (supported by building in evaluation from the very start). The commitments mean that you need to be prepared to build relationships with people through evidence gathering as well as engaging them in the process, being curious and adaptable as new information becomes available, and seeking to truly understand the impact of policies on children and young people.

Table 8.2 Look at the evidence

	Element B: Look at the evidence
Stage 1: Why does this matter?	**How do you know it matters?** • Consider future scenarios and evidence from across the system • Ask 'what if' questions • Expand the types of evidence • Build processes to store and retrieve evidence
Stage 2: How will you address it?	**How do you know your approach is viable?** • Find where and when the issue has been or is being addressed • Develop and test hypotheses • Develop and evaluate prototypes, thought experiments, and trials to try out proposals
Stage 3: How will you communicate it?	**How do you know your communications will be effective?** • Identify what people already know, understand, and value • Identify past communication that was effective • Map and share the concerns across the system
Stage 4: How will you evaluate it and move forward?	**How will you make good decisions?** • Map the evidence and methods against the success criteria • Map evidence gathering against the evaluation timeline • Identify and carry out research that might give unexpected results • Consider who else is collecting evidence

Element C: Be transparent about decisions

A favourite question in civil service interviews is something along the lines of, 'How do you use evidence to make decisions, and what do you do when the evidence is unclear or contradictory?' Aside from the fact that the evidence is *always* imperfect, the standard answer invariably ends up relying on the importance of exercising judgement and citing appropriate caveats.

This is not a bad thing in itself. Policy-making and implementation has to be about exercising judgement – albeit in a way that makes as much use of expertise and evidence as possible – precisely because there is never a single, right answer to any issue. But there is a general aversion to being open and honest about that fact, about being clear when and how judgement is being exercised.

More common is an attempt to hide behind a selective set of evidence to make a point without citing the contrary case and acknowledging that it has been considered. This leads to a feeling of dishonesty – and ultimately distrust – about the policy-making process that would be made better if the judgement being made was clearer. And although there may be a short-term political hit in admitting that the evidence you are making a decision on is incomplete, it is better to own that fact than ignore it.

Throughout this stage, policy-makers will need to make decisions – who to engage in the conversations, how, and when; what and how much evidence to collect; which issues to pursue and which to avoid or postpone. Some of these decisions will be easy for people to understand, obvious from the conversations and the evidence. Others will be led by political or financial constraints, or the limits of time. Some will be based on values and principles, which may be contested, and others on the kind of future that policy-makers envisage or want to build.

Decisions must be made about how to implement a policy, and in particular the timing of implementation, based on a thorough understanding of the likely challenges in any timetable. It should be made explicit when pace is required for non-policy-related reasons (for example, given the current academic year, any policy to be introduced at the beginning of a school year in September needs to be sufficiently advanced in time or else a delay of a year might be needed). And it should be direct at the beginning about any factors that could create risks to delivery.

In communicating decisions, it is important to be honest. To be clear, we are not saying that governments, unions, think tanks, and pressure groups are deliberately lying, but in the current system decisions appear fully formed with all the arguments behind them. There is an understandable urge to present information in the best possible light to push a particular agenda, which may help in the short-term political back-and-forth, but comes at a cost for the implementation of a policy and the trust of those leading it. So you should not just think about how best to get your point of view across, but be prepared to be open to sharing difficult and critical information, making clear that in most cases, the choices are not straightforward. Part of the aim of being transparent and open throughout the process is to commit to building relationships of trust where all are open to learning from each other.

Table 8.3 Be transparent about decisions

	Element C: Be transparent about decisions
Stage 1: Why does this matter?	**Why have you chosen this issue now?** • Set out the ideas that were discarded, and why • Clarify your values and long-term vision • Be clear about how your decisions relate to your constituents • Be clear why you chose these people and this evidence
Stage 2: How will you address it?	**Why have you chosen this approach?** • Set out approaches that were considered or tried and discarded, and why • Identify constraints – funding, resourcing, staffing, etc. that affect the decision • Map potential impacts and mitigations
Stage 3: How will you communicate it?	**How will you share the judgements made?** • Be clear if there is information that is too sensitive to share • Be prepared for criticism
Stage 4 How will you evaluate it and move forward?	**How have you chosen to evaluate?** • Be clear about your choice of success criteria and research questions • Identify the other factors (financial, political...) that influenced decisions and next steps • Be clear about the balance between present and future needs

All organisations involved in the policy-making process have their own aims, values, and constituents to satisfy. This too is not a bad thing. But it is important to recognise the agenda underpinning the decisions made and to acknowledge openly the constraints within which decisions have been taken.

There are risks to this approach, although people disagreeing with you is not one of them. More of an issue are those who are not interested in engaging in good faith and seek to act as spoilers rather than constructive critics. You are never going to be able to completely stop this behaviour – people are people after all – but there are ways to mitigate it. First, it is important to be clear about the parameters of discussion, what is up for debate and what is off the table, for whatever reasons. Second, be clear when conversations should be confidential and when they can be shared, and hold people to account if they break that confidence, making clear that confidential discussions are there to protect all members of any group so they feel they can speak freely. Third, be prepared to accept the power dynamics at play and develop a thick skin as needed. Those who hold decision-making power will need to accept that they are more likely to be criticised. In particular, do not give in to defensiveness, especially not a defensiveness that leads to attacking your critics.

Chapter summary

• A new way of making policy needs to take place in a changed culture: one that prioritises building relationships, learning, and focusing on children and young people.

- Within this, the policy-making toolkit weaves together four stages and three elements.
- The four stages – points of decision – focus on asking why the issue matters, how to address it, how to communicate it, and how to evaluate and move on.
- The three elements describe the processes – involving people, engaging with research, and being transparent about decisions.
- Each stage and element has within it a number of questions to help shape the thinking needed for better policy-making.

Notes

1 An idea suggested by Michael Gove, www.bbc.co.uk/news/uk-politics-64803947.
2 www.imdb.com/title/tt0751809/characters/nm0248844
3 www.imdb.com/title/tt0751809/characters/nm0248844
4 www.instituteforgovernment.org.uk/comment/hs2-delays-infrastructure-planning
5 www.gov.uk/guidance/teaching-and-leadership-innovation-fund-programmes-for-teachers-and-school-leaders
6 www.gov.uk/government/publications/teaching-and-leadership-innovation-fund-tlif-evaluation-and-project-reports
7 www.psychologytoday.com/gb/basics/groupthink. See also Anthony King and Ivor Crewe, *The Blunders of Our Governments* (Oneworld Publications, 2014).
8 www.nao.org.uk/reports/the-building-schools-for-the-future-programme-renewing-the-secondary-school-estate/

9   The toolkit in action

Having worked through the stages, elements, and commitments in Chapter 8, the toolkit begins to look like Figure 9.1.

A toolkit of course must have practical application and so this final chapter explores its use in addressing one of the most pressing issues for our current education system. Few people would disagree that teacher recruitment and retention is the key issue to address over the next few years. It has in fact been a key issue for a long time, and seems clearly to fit the definition of a 'wicked' problem. As Sinéad McBrearty, CEO of Education Support, makes clear: 'If we can fix the retention crisis, we will also fix the recruitment crisis. We're not just trying to rebuild the lives of teachers; we're trying to rebuild the reputation of the profession'.[1] The point of this chapter is not to provide the solution: we recognise that

	ELEMENTS		
STAGES	A. Involve the right people	B. Look at the evidence	C. Be transparent about decisions
1. Why does this matter?	Who does this matter to?	How do you know it matters?	Why have you chosen this issue now?
2. How will you address it?	Who will be part of addressing it?	How do you know your approach is viable?	Why have you chosen this approach?
3. How will you communicate it?	Who needs to know what, when, and how?	How do you know your communications will be effective?	How will you share the judgements made?
4. How will you evaluate it and move forward?	Who can tell you what's worked and what hasn't?	How will you make good decisions?	How have you chosen to evaluate?

Figure 9.1 The Better Policy-Making Toolkit in full

DOI: 10.4324/9781032651057-10

part of our current problem is that solutions are developed in isolation from those involved and from consideration of issues across the system. Instead, we have set out how the toolkit could be used for a deeper exploration of the issues and their possible solutions. Working through the toolkit, we will also have in mind the culture that we are also trying to build: of relationships, learning, and a focus on children and young people.

Stage 1: Why does this matter?

Table 9.1 Why does this matter?

Stage 1	*A: Involve the right people*	*B: Look at the evidence*	*C: Be transparent about decisions*
Why does this matter?	*Who does this matter to?*	*How do you know it matters?*	*Why have you chosen this issue now?*

There is no single solution to the recruitment and retention crisis. Working through Stage 1, we begin to understand why: there are many reasons why it matters, and each will need different ideas to resolve them. It is, at its simplest, a question of numbers. There are not enough teachers in the system; the Department for Education has missed its recruitment targets for many years, and more teachers are leaving each year. The numbers are not quite that simple of course – there are different problems for different subjects, different school phases, and different areas of the country. But the question we have posed is 'why does it matter that we cannot recruit, or retain, enough teachers?' Answers include:

- Pupils are missing out on specialist subject teaching, which impacts on their outcomes.
- Teacher vacancies and turnover makes it more difficult for teachers to know their pupils, which impacts on learning and behaviour.
- Vacancy rates make school leaders' jobs increasingly stressful as they try to run their schools.
- There are fewer teachers for children with special needs, which impacts on their right to education.
- Losing experienced teachers means not enough growth and development in the profession, leading to a profession that is 'uncertain' of its worth and increasingly unconfident.

Alongside the general question, we might also want to be asking, 'why does it matter that we can't recruit or retain enough teachers who are Black or minority ethnic, who are men (particularly in primary and early years), who are disabled or neurodiverse, who are from working-class backgrounds?'

Perhaps it's because:

- We are missing a wealth of experience that would improve pupils' outcomes.
- Recruiting from these backgrounds would bring in more teachers.
- It suggests that entry to teaching or access to promotion is not equitable.

We can come at this from a different angle and ask, 'What would it look like if there were enough teachers?' This raises questions about what we mean by 'enough'. Do we need a certain number of teachers:

- to suit the pupil:teacher ratios we think are best
- to teach in the ways we think are best: secondary subject specialists and primary generalists
- to be in school while pupils are there – and we expect all pupils to be in school across a defined school day and year.

Ultimately, asking why it matters prompts us to confront the idea that teaching is not viewed as an attractive, long-term career, and that something about the culture and practices of teaching, or of schools, needs to change. It also makes us question our assumptions of what teaching should look like or how teachers should work.

Element A: Involve the right people – who does this matter to?

This is of course a small range of possible reasons why the issue matters, and in order to set out a fuller picture but also to begin to narrow down the issues we want to address, we need to involve the right people. Who are the people to whom this issue matters? It is obvious that it matters to teachers and school leaders, and also to their unions and other representative bodies. But a teacher supply crisis matters to children, young people, and their parents and carers; to the wider community – particularly if pupils are at home or on the streets; and to employers.

It matters to different groups of people on different timelines too: it matters now for teachers under pressure to teach unfamiliar subjects and cover unfamiliar classes, for pupils taught by many different teachers who don't know them or the subject in depth, for parents who see their children unhappy or who are fighting for the right education for their children's needs, and for employers who see parents juggling their work with the needs of their children. It also matters for the future of the profession, of the economy, and of society. After all, most jobs available now and in the future rely on teachers, and an open and just society needs people with knowledge and skills who have learnt to get along with each other; all of which relies on a functioning education system.

The people, the questions, and the methods of engagement will be different as we look at different timelines. Teachers can talk about why they join and stay in the profession – and why they might leave. They can identify issues of conditions and cultures, and could be engaged through consultation, like Nicky Morgan's Workload Challenge.[2] It will also be worth talking to those who have recently left and to engage with those who have never thought of becoming teachers, or who have made conscious decisions not to join, through groups in universities or different kinds of employment.

Longer-term issues, of what teaching or teachers' working lives could look like, are better addressed through conversations. While teachers should be involved, it should be broadened out to other professions, as well as academics, think tanks, and other organisations that have been considering these issues. It should involve parents and carers, children and young people to understand what matters to them about their teachers and their school experience. We should engage what design thinkers call the 'extreme users' here too. For these purposes, this may be those with expertise in SEND and alternative provision or those who work in or attend small schools and across large MATs. It should include those from Black and minority ethnic backgrounds, those who have been teaching a long time and those who are new.

Of course, there is a huge time commitment here, and it is not feasible for every policy issue to be addressed in this way. But we have been trying to 'solve' teacher recruitment and retention for decades. We believe it is time to think more broadly about the issue. It is also clear that there are relationships to be built here: teachers are frustrated by the lack of public understanding of their role and the calls for change from politicians that imply that they are not good enough. Working through the issues together, building relationships of respect and an understanding of the value of teachers' work, may also ultimately be part of the solution.

Element B: Look at the evidence – how do you know it matters?

Engaging with a broad range of people will give a great deal of anecdotal evidence about why the issue matters and, collected and analysed carefully, can build a picture of how, why, where, and to whom it matters across the country. But people's experiences and their arguments will be contextual and biased, and it is important to build a broader understanding of the issue.

There is already a wealth of data about teacher supply. We know, nationally, how many teachers there are, how many join and leave the profession, how long teachers stay. It is less clear what the issues are locally – how many schools are struggling to recruit, how many teachers are teaching outside their specialisms. These numbers are important, particularly for short-term fixes, and will be helpful as we narrow down the issue and begin to think about success criteria, but they don't tell us why there is a problem. They also don't answer the questions of how many teachers we need and how many we need in particular subjects or in particular locations. For that, we need to be asking those deeper questions about what teaching looks like. We need to look for evidence about what children and young people need at different stages of education: more teachers in the early years or at A level? More teachers with SEND specialisms or smaller classes so that children with SEND are properly included?

This is a point at which future scenarios could be helpful. The OECD has developed four scenarios for education that have very different implications for teachers,[3] including more personalised teaching, greater use of digital learning platforms, schools as learning 'hubs' involving a greater variety of 'teachers', and a move away from teaching as we know it as learners begin to choose where and how to learn. The World Economic Forum takes those scenarios and envisages 'modernising' the current system,[4] 'transforming' it, and schools 'disappearing' altogether. Alternatively, we may want to build our own pictures, extrapolating from trends in AI and other technology, the increasing focus on technical and vocational learning, or the impact of climate change or poverty.

If we need more teachers, we should also ask where they might come from. Who are the sorts of people we are looking to attract and where are they currently working, what roles are they training for? Is there evidence of a large enough pool of people tempted by 'caring' roles to focus our efforts on attracting them into teaching; where are the numbers of specialists – software engineers, accountants, industrial scientists – who could become subject teachers? What if we are already recruiting the most we can? The evidence may suggest that we need to change teaching in order to operate within these constraints.

We will need to look at evidence from employment outside teaching. Matthew Taylor's report 'Good Work' suggests that quality will mean different things to people at different stages of their careers,[5] but that it may include opportunities for fulfilment and development and to have a voice in the workplace. Research from McKinsey and others suggests employees want their work to have meaning and their employers to have a purpose.[6] Teaching would seem to have those things, and so we should look for evidence about how they engage people,

These are not questions with easy answers. But there are people considering these kinds of questions and building evidence to support their answers. In defining the issues, it is important to engage with a broad range of evidence and build learning relationships with those who are involved. This could include academic and practitioner research, evidence from 'What Works' agencies,[7] ideas from across the world and from the other UK nations. Organisations involved in place-based research, or in early years and childcare, further and higher education, may offer important lessons to consider. Thinking beyond the education system will also be vital: we know that more people become teachers in a recession when the number and security of jobs decreases, but how is teacher supply impacted by numbers of healthcare and social workers, the increase in physical and mental health needs, and child and family poverty?

Many of these will be questions that have been considered in the past and will be considered again in the future. It is important to look at evidence that has already been collected, and to talk to those who have been involved in discussing and addressing these issues before. It is also vital to develop processes to collate the evidence collected in the present, and systems to ensure it is kept and made available when the issues arise next time.

Element C: Be transparent about decisions – why have you chosen this issue now?

Thinking around this issue must be focused on long-term planning rather than short-term solutions. We believe that policy-making needs to step, at least briefly, outside the constraints of the current system. We need to move from the important and urgent business of finding enough teachers for the system we have now and into the important but not urgent longer-term thinking that gets swallowed up by our need to fight fires.[8] This is a decision that needs to be transparent.

Decisions will be based on beliefs about education – perhaps that all young people must learn maths and physics to a certain standard but can choose whether to learn music or design technology; beliefs about employment – whether young people need certain skills and knowledge rather than others, or whether passing exams is more important than taking part in work experience; beliefs about learning and teaching – whether children learn best when they progress through school with others their own age, grouped in discrete subjects and perhaps by ability. These are usually decisions that are so ingrained within the system that we don't even think of them as decisions: they are just the way things are.

Decisions about the people we choose to involve will be led by our focus on the future. Often in thinking about recruitment and retention, we talk to teacher supply experts, teachers in 'outstanding schools', and organisations involved in pay and conditions. Choosing to involve different people may lead to concerns about the long-term agenda or values. Our vision for the future may need to involve serious change to the education system, and being transparent in both the vision and the choice of questions we seek to address will help to clarify our thinking as well as offer the opportunity for others to ask questions and to disagree.

With an eye to the commitment to increase learning, transparency about decisions at this stage may well open up much deeper issues that could be explored. It should also be led by a commitment to relationships: transparency at this stage is a step towards building trust, being honest about the reasons for decisions and being open to further exploration, even if that is likely to be further down the line.

Stage 2: How will you address it?

Table 9.2 How will you address it?

Stage 2	A: Involve the right people	B: Look at the evidence	C: Be transparent about decisions
How will you address it?	*Who will be part of addressing it?*	*How do you know your approach is viable?*	*Why have you chosen this approach?*

Deciding how to address an issue depends on being clear about the issue to be addressed. With a problem as complex as teacher recruitment and retention it is clear that a range of interventions is needed, some of which are short term in order to fix today's problems and some of which are much longer term. As we have set out already, policy-makers are, perhaps understandably, focused on short-term crisis management: this toolkit is intended to prompt a rebalancing as well as to find short-term 'solutions' that can build towards a longer-term plan.

Evidence from previous policy initiatives, and indeed from across the world, also suggests that it is very difficult to recruit increasing numbers of teachers. For the purposes of this chapter, we have made the decision to consider how we might retain more of those we currently have, in order to illustrate the operation of the toolkit. We will need to spend some time defining the issue more closely, deciding whether this is because it is expensive to keep training teachers who leave within a few years, for example, or because it is better for children and the profession to have more experienced teachers. Considering how to address each of these, and others, will help us to come up with different possible solutions. Helpfully, some of those ideas may well be useful for both retention and recruitment, in particular the idea of making teaching a more attractive career.

Even narrowing down our ideas in this way will open up a range of options, both short- and long term. At this stage, it is important to come up with as many ideas as possible – even those that are not feasible may have elements within them that are worth considering.

There are many ideas that could make a difference in the short- to medium term:

- Increasing pay.
- Improving opportunities for flexible working.
- Reducing workload – for example, setting a maximum working week or cutting five hours a week.
- Increasing non-contact time to make more time for planning and for professional development.
- Improving resources – better school buildings, classroom resources, staffrooms.
- More textbooks and online lessons to cut the time teachers need to plan and find resources.
- More support for pupils – teaching assistants in schools, 'team around the child or family' to support outside school.
- Better career pathways for teachers.
- Improving accountability procedures and measures.
- Changing the curriculum so that it is broader or less intensive.
- Changing recruitment, qualifications, or training.

Looking to the longer term, there may be ways in which teaching itself can change in order to be more attractive:

- Teachers could have more freedom to plan a curriculum to suit their context and pupils.
- Education could become more project based, with pupils empowered and supported to follow their own pathways.
- More focus on technical and vocational learning could lead to a wider range of people involved in teaching – including employers.
- Teaching as a career could involve being part of policy development, community engagement, or building links with employers.

- Teachers could be expected to be part of subject, research, or employment networks, improving their academic knowledge and skills or spending regular time in research or other jobs.

It is important to map these possibilities across the education system. Giving teachers more freedom to develop curriculum or offering pupils more choice would likely need changes to assessment and accountability, while increases to opportunities for professional development could need work to ensure the quality and impact of professional development and might lead to demands for better career pathways and more pay. It is also worth trying to map possible outcomes over time: a focus on developing textbooks or online lessons might lead to better teaching and reduced workload, or it could reduce teacher professionalism by allowing less-qualified people to deliver someone else's lessons. Of course, it is impossible to know for certain what the outcome will be, but identifying the possibilities allows for better conversations and more focused evaluations.

It is equally important to map across different parts of the system. Increasing the support for pupils and families by developing a 'team around the child' will involve finding more healthcare and social workers, more support for families in poverty, and more welfare and attendance support. Most of this is outside the control of the Department for Education and has its own constraints and limitations.

The timing of implementation is also key, and mapping interventions against other things going on in the system will raise more questions to address. There may be changes planned to curriculum or qualifications, teacher training, or ways in which teachers can be recruited from abroad, all of which could impact on timings. Building a long-term plan will allow for gradual changes that will build relationships and offer time to learn and reflect on what makes a sustainable teaching profession while also giving a much better idea of when there might be capacity in the system for particular interventions.

Element A: Involve the right people – who will be part of addressing it?

It may be that the same people are involved at Stage 2 as at Stage 1. But different groups and different methods of engagement should also be considered. As possible solutions are identified and mapped, it is vital to continue to check understandings. There are questions to be asked about what would make teaching more attractive, and whether there are different interventions for different phases and subjects or teachers' backgrounds and career stages, for example.

Some of this can be done through consultation, particularly where there are reasonably open questions, perhaps a range of options to be ranked in order. Setting out how to address the issue could also helpfully involve developing prototypes and thought experiments, involving those who will implement interventions in thinking through different ideas or developing trials of small parts of an intervention. In order to consider a maximum working hours contract, it should be possible to bring teachers and leaders together to think through the implications of this: to identify those things that would be impossible to manage and those things that would have to change in order to make the job possible. It might also be possible to find some schools willing to try maximum hours contracts for a period of time and who can record difficulties and benefits. There may be schools that have tried different ways of cutting the hours worked, and those should definitely be part of conversations about how to address the issue.

It is vital that 'the right people' includes those who will find the proposals difficult to implement as well as those who have been involved in these kinds of changes before, through national policy changes or local interventions. We need to involve those who will be impacted by policy changes as well as those who will implement them: when changes are made to teachers' working hours it is often teaching assistants who pick up the slack. Governors have oversight of teaching and an external perspective on ways of working, which could be very helpful. Changes to working hours, or to the ways in which teachers work, may well have an impact on parents and will definitely impact children and young people – they should all be involved in the thinking.

Good relationships between teacher unions, government, and other organisations will be needed. It is neither possible nor desirable for government to manage all of the ideas, the trialling, and the discussions needed at this stage, but many other organisations may already be involved or could be invited to support the work. If one of the possible answers is to increase time for professional development, the Chartered College of Teaching or National Institute of Teaching could each be involved in developing and trialling possible ideas. The unions will have a strong understanding of working conditions and the possible impact of different ideas, as well as ready access to members across the profession. In thinking about longer-term changes to teaching it will be worth involving those outside the education sector. If we want to increase links between teachers, their subject or research community, employers, or the local community then each of these groups need to be involved in the thinking. Each will also need to be committed to learning from others rather than shutting down possibilities that don't match their own answers. In particular, we believe that there is a place for some level of co-production, engaging semi-permanent groups of individuals and organisations to develop ways of addressing the issues, particularly for the long term.

Some form of social partnership would allow conversations to take place confidentially between government and the unions, particularly about potentially controversial issues such as the six-week summer holiday or the length of the school day. While there is evidence of the impact of these on learning and on family life, conversations about changing them move very quickly into defence of teachers' conditions, their need for holiday, and for sufficient time away from the classroom to carry out all the other teaching-related duties. Behind closed doors, with a focus on the long term and with sufficient trust between unions and government, it could be possible to build better understanding of the concerns of teachers and their unions about professional status and working hours. A commitment to learning and maintaining relationships could lead to fruitful conversations about finding ways to extend the time pupils are engaged in learning which does not extend teachers' working hours or undermine their professionalism.

Element B: Look at the evidence – how do you know your approach is viable?

We know from research what makes teaching unattractive. What happens though is that we take an idea, for example that high workload makes teaching unattractive, and we attempt to resolve it – by cutting working hours, listing tasks that teachers do not need to do, and cutting down on the amount of data collection required by government. All of these are important but they do not necessarily get to the heart of the matter. At times, there are calls to consider evidence of what leads to the long working hours and unnecessary tasks, and then the response may be to reform the accountability system so that there is less data to collect and to reform Ofsted so that accountability does not have such high stakes. We might consider evidence of what makes teaching less attractive when compared with other workplaces, which could lead to increasing pay or promoting more flexible working, allowing teachers to do their planning at home or offering part-time work and job shares.

We find different answers when we look for evidence of what makes teaching attractive. Research shows that teachers want to make a difference for their pupils, to encourage them to continue learning, to develop a love for their subject, and to grow into well-rounded adults who will make a positive contribution to society. Teachers who continue to learn, who are supported to improve their practice, and who work in cultures that enable them to grow are much more likely to stay in the profession. Addressing this is a lot more complex. The hypotheses we may want to test include different ideas of why there is not enough of this in the system or whether engaging teachers in policy-making, and in different networks of expertise, would encourage retention and make teaching attractive to different kinds of people.

Engaging the right people will bring out more ideas, and there will be academics and practitioner researchers who have developed further evidence. Conversations about what is good about teaching will prompt questions about what teaching could look like, what do we want more of? This allows us to consider evidence from those places where teaching is oversubscribed and where teachers want to stay.

The question then becomes how to use what we know to address the declining numbers of teachers. Are there ideas and interventions that have worked in different countries, at different times in our past, or in particular areas of the country? Is there evidence from particular groups of schools, MATs, or local authority projects? Are there other professions that have addressed similar issues? In particular, we may find ideas that work with particular groups of teachers – those who have been in the same school for a number of years, those who work with children with autism, Black teachers. This is not to suggest that once we have identified the issue to address we can find a ready-made solution. But with a commitment to learning, we can use the evidence from elsewhere to question the assumptions we hold, to identify gaps in the evidence, and commission work to fill those gaps.

Element C: Be transparent about decisions – why have you chosen this approach?

It should be abundantly clear that we cannot address every issue that undermines teacher retention. It is also impossible to address all the important issues at the same time. In looking at implementing solutions, there will be clear funding constraints: there is both a finite amount of money available in education budgets and a limited amount that the general public will find acceptable to spend. Choosing to spend money on teachers will mean spending less on other important parts of the education system or it will mean spending less on health, policing, or defence. These are political decisions, and it is important to be transparent at the start about what is available so that expectations are realistic.

We should also expect transparency about the assumptions being made. If we spend money on bursaries for secondary teachers, there is an assumption that there are sufficient teachers in primary or early years education and enough special needs teachers. These assumptions may not be correct, and they may not have been consciously reached.

There should also be transparency about policies that we believe should not be changed, even if changing them might lead to better outcomes in this situation. This is true for government who might decide that keeping the current accountability system is important to maintain a focus on standards, even though changing accountability could have a big impact on teacher workload. It is true for unions who might decide that continuing to increase the numbers of teachers (and therefore their members) is important even if reducing the numbers could allow more money to be spent on increasing teacher wages.

Other decisions will be based on the kind of future we expect, or want. Decisions may be based on a view that we will need more scientists in the future to develop and implement green technologies or to mitigate the worst effects of climate change. The rise of AI could mean that we need to retain fewer teachers. Perhaps the rise in poverty and inequality will mean we need more pastoral care, mental health specialists, or behaviour support. Or we may look at the increasing trend for workers to change jobs and careers many times over a lifetime and decide that we should find ways to make it possible to move between teaching and different jobs or careers, perhaps many times. Alternatively, governments could decide to prioritise raising families out of poverty, meeting needs early, and putting money into initiatives outside teaching that will have an enormous effect on the work that teachers do. All of these might mean spending less on teaching but could have a huge impact on teacher retention.

Stage 3: How will you communicate it?

Table 9.3 How will you communicate it?

Stage 3	A: Involve the right people	B: Look at the evidence	C: Be transparent about decisions
How will you communicate it?	*Who needs to know what, when, and how?*	*How do you know your communications will be effective?*	*How will you share the judgements made?*

At this point, we will narrow the policy suggestions to consider two ideas that could improve teacher retention: reducing workload by capping teachers' working hours and increasing teachers' engagement in decisions that impact on their working lives through greater involvement in policy-making. These are quite different, and possibly mutually exclusive, suggestions. They are not suggestions that we have chosen because we think they are the right ones, but because they will help us to illustrate how the toolkit can be used in Stages 3 and 4.

To begin with, it will be important to clarify the messages. Each of these decisions will need a different sort of messaging: capping teachers' working hours is a contractual issue while engaging teachers in decision-making is more about winning hearts and minds. Both require teachers to change the ways they work, one in order to cut their overall hours and the other in order to find space for other important aspects of their work. The first may be easier to communicate to an overburdened workforce, while the second needs to appeal to a different vision of teaching.

Both would benefit from reframing how we talk about workload. Teaching has always required hard work and long hours, there is always more that teachers can do to improve lessons or individual support for pupils, and they have always had to make choices about when to stop, when it is 'good enough'. What has increased dissatisfaction is the proliferation of work that doesn't make a difference to teaching, the planning that is about writing everything down for someone else, the data collection that is to fulfil a requirement. But there is also still a suspicion that teachers have short days and long holidays. The idea that teaching needs to change because teachers work too hard does not invoke sympathy among those whose jobs have also become busier and less secure. If changes to teaching might cost money, or lead to teachers spending fewer hours with pupils, there may be little support from parents or from politicians who claim to represent the views of parents in their constituencies.

Communication is in part about telling a story and it needs a focus on the audience. The broad message may be about how the change is good for society or the economy. For parents, it needs to focus on what they expect for their children, which is often based on their own experiences of school. If they believe that their child needs to see the same teacher every day, changes that cut that contact will be unpopular. Instead, it needs to explain why the change is better for children. Capping the hours worked will mean teachers who are less stressed; other changes will be needed to ensure that lesson quality will not drop. Teachers engaged in policy-making will mean that the system will better meet the needs of children; again, other communications will need to address how 'my' child will benefit and not lose out.

Communication should also include messages about the process of change. In particular, there will need to be reassurances that small-scale trialling of different ways of doing things will not impact negatively on pupil learning.

There is more to giving clear messages than presenting the facts. It is important to think about the values that will shine through the messaging. In addressing teacher retention, communication needs to demonstrate the importance of teaching, show respect for those in the profession, and build up the idea of teaching as a worthwhile professional career. It needs to steer clear of any suggestion that teachers are 'not good enough'. For teachers themselves, each of these messages also needs to explain how change will support their professional identity, help them to balance their lives, and enable them to thrive.

It is important that communication is credible. Teachers, and others, will not believe a policy to cut working hours if it is communicated at the end of the week or in school holidays. Nor will they believe a commitment to involve them in important decisions if it comes alongside another idea for compulsory tooth-brushing. Credibility is also about being seen to understand the issues and the realities of day-to-day life in schools – a policy that cuts teacher workload will not be credible if it relies on large numbers of support staff or collaborative working that is difficult in a small school.

Element A: Involve the right people – who needs to know what, when, and how?

Teachers may respond to these policy ideas, initially at least, with hollow laughter: at the idea of adding yet more to their responsibilities or at one more 'workload initiative'. Communication needs to be at least two way, between policy-makers and the profession, to involve those who are excited by the possibility and those who think it mad, with each open to listening and learning. As policy is developed, messaging can be created to meet the concerns of each.

Those who are engaged in trialling different ways of cutting working hours, or being involved in policy-making, will need to be involved in developing messages to communicate. They will understand the frustrations others will experience, as well as the satisfaction of successful practices. Communication will need to be multidimensional, in order to bring in the views and expertise of others inside and outside the system, and to offer explanations of decisions that are tailored to their expectations and interest. Teachers and policy-makers can learn from initiatives introduced in the health service, teachers can explore how some of those ideas could work in schools, and their expertise and reflections could inform both policy-makers and employers.

Policies are often communicated as stand-alone interventions, making it sound as if these are the silver bullet that will solve the problem. Thinking longer term allows announcements like these to form part of a plan, balancing simple ideas to address immediate concerns with complex policy thinking around the deeper issues. Capping working hours could form part of the conversations about what is important to teaching, which could lead into conversations about how teaching itself could change. It also allows the process of engagement to form part of the communication.

Involving the right people may be about trialling different messages to see what resonates. Messages will be heard differently by different groups: it is easy to make it sound as if the problem of teacher workload and wellbeing is the fault of head-teachers or that the solution is to increase the workload of teaching assistants. Testing communications with different groups will help to demonstrate those kinds of problems early on.

There will be times when the values of different people in the process clash – some may believe that teaching is a calling and that cutting working hours makes the contract more important than the pupils; others may believe that the importance of their role lies in their work with pupils so that cutting that time, even if it is to become involved in wider decisions about policy, undermines those values. Clashing values may make policies very difficult to implement. Focusing on building relationships should mean approaching conversations with honesty and clarity, including talking about values.

Element B: Look at the evidence – how do you know your communications will be effective?

To start, you will need to set out success criteria for your communication: will you count how many people heard or have acted on the messages, or is it more important that particular people or groups are engaged? Communication at different stages of the policy process and with different people will need to be evaluated differently: for a policy that will cut teachers' working hours, there will need to be communication at the point of implementation that explains the system to teachers, school leaders, parents, and pupils. Each will have a different purpose: to develop in-school processes that will cut working hours; to ensure that teachers are not under pressure to work beyond their contracted hours; to make sure that pupils and parents understand the limitations on teachers' working hours. Each will provide different evidence. To be clear, this is not evidence of whether the policy is successful, but whether the communication has got to the right people with the right messages.

There is plenty of data to analyse to understand whether people open emails or click on links, which can give some indication of what leads people to engage. It is worth considering what we can learn from different ways of communicating. Some seem designed to antagonise, to set up one set of values against another, one form of teaching against another, or to suggest that there is one right answer and that those who disagree are against change. With its focus on relationships, this toolkit leads towards communication that builds communities and encourages dialogue. This is not to say that there is no room for argument, but this is argument that opens up space for learning, not argument to score points.

Finding evidence of what is important to those who will hear the messaging, what they already know, and what they will need to make the changes being proposed will make communication easier. Headteachers will need to hear how they can continue to manage their schools if teachers' contracts change or teachers are engaged in policy-making processes; teachers will need to understand how to manage the impact on their pupils, how the change might impact on their career progression, or more practically how they are expected to record their working hours. The success of these communications may be measured by talking to (a sample of) heads and teachers or their representatives.

It is also worth considering the evidence used to underpin the communication: is that evidence credible, can it apply to a range of settings and individuals, and does it come from a number of different studies or just one preferred source?

Element C: Being transparent about decisions – how will you share the judgements made?

This toolkit requires humility in communication – nobody has the right answer because there is no single right answer. Instead, we are all working towards a better, more attractive teaching profession and each strand of a solution is moving us in that direction. Proper evaluation will enable us to course-correct even when an intervention turns out to be unhelpful, and these are all decisions that need to be transparently communicated. It is still likely that these decisions will be derided as U-turns, a government lacking in direction or expertise, or a waste of money and time. But communicating them as part of a long-term plan to find answers, rather than the solution that will fix the problem, can buy space for learning.

It will be important to communicate clearly what has been learnt when a decision is made to stop an intervention. If setting a limit on working hours turns out to be too difficult, it is important for relationships of trust that the decision not to continue does not suggest that it is the fault of teachers or headteachers. There must be an opportunity to reflect, in order to be able to communicate underlying reasons why it doesn't work in the current system and suggestions for issues that could now be explored. If engagement in policy-making is impossible without employing more teachers, that needs to be communicated in ways that don't imply that it could have worked if the government had enough commitment to the process.

It is also vital to be clear where confidentiality has been agreed or where information is too sensitive to share. It may be that either of our two policy ideas could work if there could be agreement to extend the number of weeks worked, but confidential conversations identified major difficulties that could not be overcome. It may be that those conversations cannot be communicated, but agreement could be reached about a form of words that all parties can use to communicate the decision and the sensitivities that underpin it.

Stage 4: How will you evaluate it and move forward?

Table 9.4 How will you evaluate it and move forward?

Stage 4	A: Involve the right people	B: Look at the evidence	C: Be transparent about decisions
How will you evaluate it and move forward?	Who can tell you what's worked and what hasn't?	How will you make good decisions?	How have you chosen to evaluate?

Evaluation, including success criteria and evaluation methods, needs to be built in at the beginning of the process. In terms of addressing teacher retention there are some obvious criteria: fewer teachers leaving. But we may have decided to focus on particular locations with greater teacher turnover or on retaining teachers at a particular age or career stage. Evaluation may show us that our particular solutions don't work in these instances, but that they could work in other areas.

Alternatively, our evaluation might involve the detail of the policies themselves: could capping working hours at 40 hours a week be easier to implement than a smaller limit, and could that also retain similar numbers of teachers? Could involving 1% of teachers in sortition processes, or 1% of schools in design labs, be easier to implement and be better at retaining teachers than larger (or smaller) numbers?

Processes should also be developed to evaluate the impact of these policies across the system and the feedback between these policies and different parts of the system. How will changes to working hours, or working practices, interact with the accountability framework? How will retaining more teachers impact on the numbers of initial teacher training places needed? What might be the consequences on school budgets of having to pay more for more experienced teachers? Answers to these questions may not be immediately apparent, but processes will need to be put in place to ensure that they are not forgotten over time.

The less concrete the criteria the harder it will be to measure, but it is usually the case that more important measures of success are less concrete, and as with all assessments it is better to try to evaluate the success of those things we value rather than those things which are easy to measure. The ultimate measure of success is an oversubscribed, rejuvenated profession, and while it is possible to show that fewer teachers are leaving the profession than in previous years, it is much harder to identify what we mean by a 'rejuvenated profession'. A focus on building relationships within the process will also lead us to want to see better public understanding of and respect for teaching.

The purpose of evaluation though is not necessarily to say that we have solved the problem, particularly not an issue as complex as teaching. Instead, it is to understand what is working and what still needs to change. So, it is right that setting, and changing, success criteria leads us to ask ever more focused questions that will feed into the ongoing review of policy to improve teacher retention.

Element A: Involve the right people – who can tell you what's worked and what hasn't?

People at different points of the policy process will have different experiences of benefits and problems, and it will be important to engage with those who have positive and negative experiences. It is also important to engage with people at different times in evaluating development and implementation, so mapping a timeframe for evaluation is key. There will be different questions to ask and observations to carry out with those who are implementing the policy and those who are affected, and it will be important to engage with people in both categories.

With every policy, there will be those who were enthusiastic from the start – the early adopters – and those who were sceptics. Some policies may have strong backing from a particular union or from government – which may mean that others are almost automatically opposed. It will also be important to involve experts in evaluation who have a clear and independent perspective. Involving each of these groups will need clear commitment to building relationships and being open to learning.

Element B: Look at the evidence – how will you make good decisions?

While this is described as Stage 4 in the process, considering the evidence in order to move forward should happen throughout the policy development and implementation process and will need to be planned against the development timeline. Each point of decision needs its evaluation point, although not all evidence will be formal research reports or data analysis. It is important then to understand what kind of evidence will be useful for moving forward.

Implementing a maximum working week for teachers will need evidence to show if it works. This would need early testing to find out how it could work, and what the barriers might be, with evidence perhaps from teacher timelogs, observations, and conversations, as well as understanding how headteachers, across different types and phases of schools, with different numbers of staff and pupils, are managing the complexities. These evaluations might also gather information from parents and pupils about their experiences – which will be useful for communication at later stages too. It is likely that evidence will come from both government- and union-led research, and each should be shared. As the decisions are made to continue with the project, testing will become larger-scale piloting, with bigger evaluation projects. Evaluation can also look at different parts of the system: where are there surprising impacts? Because national implementation is likely to include contract changes, a decision to implement will need to be based on very positive evaluation reports: a maximum hours contract is unlikely to be revoked quickly. So, a longer-term plan may include fixed-point evaluations but these will look at implementation and how to manage any problems and share successes. Ongoing review should consider the impact on pupil outcomes as well as on teacher (and headteacher) retention.

Providing opportunities for teachers to be engaged in policy development will need a different approach to evaluation. Early testing might need to evaluate different forms of engagement in order to decide whether to pick one or to develop a menu of options. Further piloting might consider more specifically the impact on pupils, colleagues, and others of both taking time away from the classroom and of being more involved in decisions about issues that matter, whether locally or nationally, Initially, national implementation will only impact on a small number of teachers and schools, and evaluation can be planned at fixed points: if the model of engagement is sortition, then evaluation would take place as different cohorts of teachers are selected, during their 'service' and as they return to the classroom for example, over a long period. Ongoing review should be set up in such a way that it can identify changes in teachers' attitudes to their careers, the profession, or teaching itself.

Throughout the evaluation process, focusing on children and young people will ensure that evidence is gathered both from them and about them. It is important to be clear about the impact of decisions on their outcomes, but also on their immediate experiences.

Element C: Be transparent about decisions – how have you chosen to evaluate?

Being clear about success criteria is vital from the earliest stages of the policy development process, and should have been considered as the issue was being clarified at Stage 1. If the concern is to improve international league table rankings while also changing the ways in which teachers work, success criteria and research questions will need to consider both of those issues. However, unexpected changes in other parts of the system may require different decisions to be made: a continuing decrease in people deciding to train as teachers may mean that changing working hours cannot go ahead, even though trials were successful. Each of these needs to be communicated honestly, in order to maintain trust, even though they may lead to criticism from all sides.

It is also vital to be clear about the balance between present and future needs as you evaluate: it is always difficult to choose long-term gain if there are difficulties in the short term, and it may be that headteachers' concerns about how to manage the timetable outweigh the benefits to teacher retention in the longer term of changing the way they work.

In conclusion

Policy-making is a complex and many-layered process, and this toolkit is obviously not intended to offer a checklist approach. Instead, it offers a set of questions and prompts to bring clarity to the issue, and to ensure that the right people are involved and the best evidence used along the way. It is for individual policy-makers to decide how those are chosen and to be transparent in those decisions. By focusing throughout on building relationships, being open to learning, and doing the best we can for children and young people, those processes are improved as policy-making itself improves.

Chapter summary

- The toolkit is used to explore the complex policy issue of teacher recruitment and retention.
- By following through each stage, the issues and decisions are narrowed and refined.
- Working through each process prompts questions about how processes could be used, but also how they can help to change the culture in which policy-making happens.
- The ideas suggested are not intended to be read as solutions to the problem – but to illustrate how the toolkit could be used in practice.

Notes

1 https://schoolsweek.co.uk/if-we-solve-the-retention-crisis-the-recruitment-crisis-will-follow/
2 https://assets.publishing.service.gov.uk/media/5a7f200740f0b62305b85394/RR445_-_Workload_Challenge_-_Analysis_of_teacher_consultation_responses_FINAL.pdf

3 https://web.archive.org/web/20220608211923/https://www.oecd.org/education/ceri/Brochure-Four-OECD-Scenarios-for-the-Future-of-Schooling.pdf

4 www.weforum.org/agenda/2021/01/future-of-education-4-scenarios/

5 https://assets.publishing.service.gov.uk/media/5a82dcdce5274a2e87dc35a4/good-work-taylor-review-modern-working-practices-rg.pdf

6 www.mckinsey.com/capabilities/people-and-organizational-performance/our-insights/the-great-attrition-is-making-hiring-harder-are-you-searching-the-right-talent-pools

7 For example, the Education Endowment Foundation.

8 A typical way of describing this is the 'Eisenhower Matrix' – a grid that sets out decision-making against parameters of urgency and importance, moving from neither urgent nor important through issues which are important but not urgent, urgent but not important, and into those which are both urgent and important. See, for example, www.forbes.com/sites/hillennevins/2023/01/05/how-to-get-stuff-done-the-eisenhower-matrix-aka-the-urgent-vs-the-important/

Epilogue

In this book we have tried to explore the different ways in which opinions have been shaped and how the dynamics of modern education policy-making have come into being. We have explored England's longer-term and recent history in this area, looked abroad for ideas, and challenged our own thinking before proposing a better way for education policy to be made. We make no apologies for not providing easy answers. Instead, we have focused on how better answers might be found by working differently, together.

We are under no illusions that our proposal is perfect, and we are expecting (completely justified) criticism and suggestions for improvement. But we firmly believe that – despite any flaws in detail or examples – our overall approach of increased collaboration, iteration, and longer-term thinking is essential if we are going to move beyond the entrenchment and divisiveness that characterises too much of the debate around education policy-making at the present time.

The pressure for the next government to make big and quick changes will be huge. They will be inheriting an education system suffering from years of under-funding, misplaced initiatives, and acting as a frontline service for many of the most challenging issues facing our children in modern England. Hard as it may be, the next government would do well to take a breath, to accept the scale of the challenge, and to commit – fully – to trying to respond to that challenge in a way that prioritises effectiveness over headlines, long-term improvements over short-term wins. That accepts that education is something that we all have to commit to working on together and embrace that as a strength of the English system, not a weakness to be ignored or rooted out.

Collaboration – while essential – does not mean a lack of individual responsibility. There are many thousands of people involved in shaping education policy in England today, and tens of thousands more at the sharp end of the decisions taken, working within schools, nurseries, colleges, and universities. While it might feel daunting to try to unpick the complexity in the system, we hope this book offers an understanding on where you might start. The more that people involved in education policy-making commit to and engage, to accept the need for compromise, to understand the importance of context and nuance, but to nonetheless push – relentlessly – for better, the more we can see the aspirations we have for the education system become a reality.

DOI: 10.4324/9781032651057-11

This is possible if we stop seeking enemies and taking comfort behind grand-standing and name-calling. If we have the collective courage to be vulnerable enough to admit that none of us have all the answers and that we all carry biases and baggage that need acknowledging and addressing. If we start to base policy-making on the notions of respect and trust. This is possible if we work together.

As well as the many sources of evidence cited in this book, we have many, many people we should thank, lots of whom are working behind the scenes in positions of relative anonymity in the civil service, in unions, and in agencies. Naming them all would be impossible, and many will want to retain that position of anonymity, so we will restrict ourselves to first names of some people who – we hope – recognise their contributions to this book. So, a very heartfelt thanks to: Elin, Stacy, Frances, Imogen, Graham, Caroline, Heather, Susie, Harjit, Rosie, Maeve, Geoff, Mary, Kathy, Jim, Mark, May, Kate, Amy, Jocelyn, Juliet, Jonathan, Jus-tine, Jas, Peter, Robin, Niamh, Lucy, Henry, Charlotte, Lisa, Jen, Cat, Marcus, Lauren, Maeve, Jess, Annabel, Sam, Natasha, Malcolm, Russell, Fi, Lis, Kay, Rox, Ruth, Alistair, Felicity, Corrie, Robyn, Sandra, Suzanne, Mohamed, Simon, Sarah, Matt, Chris, Sinead, Hong, Darren, Alison, Verity, Amanda, Bob, Sue, Rebecca, Victoria, Anfal, Lorna, Michelle, Tara, Gemma, David, Bethan, Dami, Michelle, Anne, Sally, Faye, Tabeetha, Naomi, Debbie, Nick, Alan, Jo, Ed, Kat, Josh, Danielle, Ali, Lesley, Martin, Kevin, Vic, Monique, Julie, Olly, Jill, Louise, Adrian, Collette, Candy, Anne, Jon, Steph, Meryl, Sheila, and Ros.

Index

For Product Safety Concerns and Information please contact our EU
representative GPSR@taylorandfrancis.com Taylor & Francis Verlag GmbH,
Kaufingerstraße 24, 80331 München, Germany

Printed and bound by CPI Group (UK) Ltd, Croydon, CR0 4YY
08/06/2025
01897002-0018